FEARLESS

ABOUT THE AUTHOR

Mama Rose is a spiritual guide, musician, mother, and author whose transformative affirmations have helped thousands overcome limiting beliefs. Drawing from her own healing journey through trauma, anxiety, and depression, she offers a compassionate framework for self-discovery and personal empowerment. Visit her at MamaRose.blog.

MAMA ROSE

FEARLESS

27 AFFIRMATIONS TO CHANGE YOUR LIFE

LLEWELLYN
WOODBURY, MINNESOTA

First Edition
First Printing, 2026

Book design by Christine Ha
Cover art by Nina Dani
Cover design by Shira Atakpu

Library of Congress Cataloging-in-Publication Data (Pending)
ISBN: 978-0-7387-8234-8

Llewellyn Publications
A Division of Llewellyn Worldwide Ltd.
2143 Wooddale Drive
Woodbury, MN 55125-2989
www.llewellyn.com

Printed in the United States of America

GPSR Representation:
UPI-2M PLUS d.o.o., Medulićeva 20, 10000 Zagreb, Croatia,
matt.parsons@upi2mbooks.hr

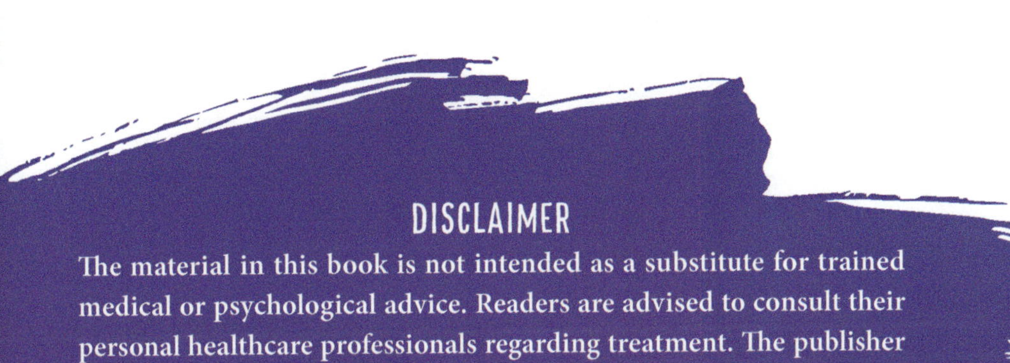

DISCLAIMER

The material in this book is not intended as a substitute for trained medical or psychological advice. Readers are advised to consult their personal healthcare professionals regarding treatment. The publisher and the author assume no liability for any injuries caused to the reader that may result from the reader's use of the content contained herein and recommend common sense when contemplating the practices described in the work.

For Maya, Beto, Thomas, and Mason. And for Nathan.

Contents

Prologue

I was an anxious child, diagnosed with obsessive-compulsive disorder at the age of five. After many years of suffering, many therapists, medications, and failed attempts at self-regulation through substances, relationships, and addictive patterns, I realized that I needed to change my thoughts. Noticing the need came before realizing that I actually had the power to do this. It seemed like an impossibly tall task. How was I supposed to change my thoughts if I didn't know what was wrong with them or what to change them into? One day, while in a clinic undergoing a minor but painful procedure, I instinctively began to make mental notes on what I saw in the room. I looked up at a box, framed with drywall in the corner near the ceiling. "Sharp line, meets another line, corner, white, dimpled paint…" I realized that I could keep myself from worrying about what was about to happen to my body if I just stayed with what was actually happening in that moment.

At that point in my life, even after years of therapy, I had never heard anyone say "the present moment." I had never heard of "mindfulness," and I had no framework for anything that would suggest my power to take control of my own thinking. I was told things like "Send the thoughts away in a jar" and "Remember that they are just thoughts and they don't have any power." I questioned how something that "didn't have any power" could be holding me as a prisoner in my own life. Thoughts had shown themselves to be the cause of my avoidant tendencies, my compulsive behaviors, and the crippling self-doubt that cast its forlorn shadow over the potential of my young life.

Then, one day I came across a prompt telling me something strikingly simple and entirely life changing. It said, "Love yourself." I was curious. I knew I wanted to love myself, but I realized that I had no training on how to do this. I could get straight A's and overwork myself with ease; in fact, it was one of the main ways I kept from drowning in the emotional waves that accompanied my anxious thoughts. I could appear to be happy and confident, I could speak well in conversation and in public, I could organize my home and my tasks, but I couldn't, for the very life of me, understand what it could possibly feel like to love myself. I wanted to find out.

I began to write messages to myself on my mirror and place little notes around my home, the same way I wrote "I want a dog" on dozens of sticky notes when I was a child and placed them everywhere that my parents would go. My mother's purse: "I want a dog"; the medicine cabinet: "I want a dog"; in between the folded towels in the kitchen drawer... You get it. Now, suddenly, wherever I looked, I was finding a new message. At first, it hurt to read "I love myself." Each time felt like a lie and was followed by a cascade of evidence as to why I should continue to believe that I was less-than-worthy of love. Everything that said, "No, don't love yourself!" came up to the surface, and I was flooded with information. I was overwhelmed by my choice to make a change. I knew I needed to establish ways to support myself if I was going to continue this work. I also knew that I *needed* to continue this work, because, despite everything I had been through, I had a bone-deep determination to prove wrong every single person, book, and article that told me I couldn't cure my OCD, overcome my PTSD, turn around my depression, and heal from my eating disorder. In other words, I had hope, and that carried me.

I wrote poetry, drew, painted, talked with friends, connected with family, found a new therapist, took a yoga class through the eating disorder recovery program I was a part of, sang, wrote music, and dreamed about a life where I was free. All the while, moments of freedom from my anxiety and depression were finding me more and more often. It seemed that every spacious moment collected a certain flavor of new energy that then magnetized more of itself into my life. I found myself reaching less and stumbling upon more. The woman next to me at the bingo hall had a bag that said "Mindfulness," a term I had just learned. The beautiful, abandoned mansion down the street from my new home that I was absolutely dying to tour just happened to sprout a chocolate shop inside it within days after I moved, and they hired me the first time I visited. Things seemed to be lining up. It was at this point that I began to realize that there was power in my intention.

Time went on. More of my dreams were liberated from the shackles of my old, patterned thoughts, and simultaneously, more energy arose from within me to pursue them. Along with it, support was coming to meet me each step of the way, sometimes cloaked in tragedy but always revealing a loving face when I learned to suspend my judgment and trust my process. It appeared that my intention to heal was enough to bypass the fact that I had no idea how to do it.

By the time I reached age twenty-seven, I had two young children, a recent separation from their father, a new partner, a lot of grief, and an expansive excitement for my future. In the spring that came after shifting into single motherhood, I lost my home. For the past six years, I had lived in a duplex with my older sister and her four children, and now, in the face of losing not only my nest but also the built-in support of my family, I was faced with the opportunity to rise to the challenge of cultivating even more inner resources. A fairly new friend of mine offered to house me, my new partner, and my children while we figured out our next moves. Two weeks before I moved out of my home and into my friend's unfinished basement, I found out I was pregnant with my third child. We moved, Covid hit the following month, and the world shut down.

George Floyd was murdered, my city was literally up in flames—the third precinct burned just blocks from my home—and on top of it all, in June of 2020, I received the hardest news of my life.

My twenty-week ultrasound revealed that my baby had serious heart defects and brain abnormalities that the doctors said, "may make him incompatible with life." They said he would for sure need heart surgery at birth, but we wouldn't know until he was born if he had grown enough brain tissue to survive or if he would even be able to handle the most basic human functions, like coordinating breathing and swallowing. The months that followed brought seemingly endless appointments, hard conversations, extreme financial stress, unexpected blessings, and a deep initiation into letting go in the face of the unknown. My ability to navigate this period of time not only with grace but also with and as love came from choosing to hold a perspective that I will share with you in this book. You, too, can take any challenges life gives you and become an empowered creator rather than a victim of your circumstances.

Life continues to be challenging, and I continue to choose gratitude for the opportunity to be living, to be growing, and to live as the love that I came here to be. In the time since I first decided to try to love myself, I have learned that the larger truth is that love is who I am. It's not something I do, but a way of being. My entire life has become not only aligned with but mobilized by that love. Now, no matter the circumstances, I remember my power to choose, and I am divinely inspired and motivated from the core of my pain, which is also the core of my heart, to share this writing with you so that you, too, can remember your power.

The affirmations that follow are the words I have spoken to myself throughout my healing journey. They have brought me through harmful self-talk and into self-awareness and an understanding of who I am that has carried me through even the darkest of nights. I continue to use these words and to create new affirmations as I go, with the understanding that every word I speak to myself is a prayer, an opportunity to commune with the Divine that exists within me.

Part 1 will teach you how to use this book. Together, we will build a framework to help you do the work of introducing new statements to your subconscious to help create fertile soil in which they can take root. There were many times that I didn't know how to move forward or even which direction was forward. I promise, however you are entering this work, you're in the right place and you're right on time. Your intention is enough to guide you to success even when you can't see how.

PART 1

The Framework for the Work

Welcome to the part of your life where you remember the power of your intention, your voice, and your choice. You are here because you are ready, and I invite you to trust this timing. As with all things, you should take this book at your own pace. I have created this book as a companion for your spiritual growth and self-discovery, and that is a lifelong process, which means you're holding a lifelong companion. These affirmations are written in such a way that they will invite your own truth to rise to the surface of your awareness in all of its layers and multidimensional beauty. What's true for you today may shift tomorrow. For this reason, I recommend that you revisit this text whenever you feel called to, bringing the same affirmations to the new you again and again.

PART 1

WHAT DOES IT MEAN TO BE FEARLESS?

Words are funny. Sometimes they hold value for us because they contain parts we can dissect—prefixes, roots, and suffixes that break down easily with meaning we can piece together like a well-kept puzzle. Other times, words are messy, a compilation of sounds born not of order but of a need to communicate something held deeply in the human psyche—sounds that invoke a feeling, a pulse of something almost beyond language. "Fearless" is one of those words that, upon initial investigation, appears to be normal. It talks about fear ("fear"), and it talks about the absence of it ("less"). But we can use it to mean something even more true. We can use it to allude to an inherent truth that doesn't mean the absence of fear at all. Instead, with the right framework, "fearless" becomes a reminder that there is a part of each of us that exists beyond fear entirely. Maybe a better word would be "fearpast" or "fearbeyond" or some other word that doesn't exist yet in the English language. But "fearless" achieves something that no other word presently does in quite the same way. It denotes the imagery and feeling of strength, it brings alive something past the ego, and it invites the soul into a position of leadership. This book reminds us of the part of ourselves that is clear and soul-directed, and it provides a guide not just to access that part once or occasionally but to restore it as our normal state of being. No longer will your fears direct the story of your life; soon, they will be restored to their rightful place in your process as messengers.

WHAT IS AN AFFIRMATION?

Affirmations are statements that we say to ourselves on purpose to affirm the parts of our identity that we would like to make stronger. There is a voice within each of us that takes the form of our thoughts and beliefs. This is the voice that we retrain to be an uplifting ally when we begin to intentionally choose what we say to ourselves. Affirmations create changes within our lives because they shift the way we view ourselves in relationship to others and the world around us. They rewire the way our consciousness works by transforming the stories we tell ourselves about why things happen and who we are. When you begin this work, you will notice that you are already talking to yourself; you are already affirming something to your subconscious at all times. However, up until now, you may not have questioned whether or not what you're affirming is supporting you or creating the patterns within your life, health, and relationships that you desire. This work is supplemental and supportive, and it's also foundational to all other types of inner work, including therapy, twelve-step programs, relationship and spiritual mentorship, and more.

THE OPTION TO JOURNAL

Writing is a way to concretely see and explore the way our inner voice is operating at any given time and to make tangible changes to the way we are speaking to ourselves. I have used writing as a tool to move myself from experiencing my life as a victim to directing my life as a creator.

Because of how impactful writing has been in my personal process, I invite you to pull writing prompts from this text and keep a journal dedicated to your journey with this book. One of my favorite tools for self-reflection is looking back at the journals I have been keeping since childhood. Not only does looking back illuminate our patterns and inspire the clarity of hindsight, but it also provides us with the opportunity to accept the past version of ourselves here and now, in the present moment, which is an incredible act of self-love.

As you move through the affirmations that I give you in this book, you will notice that you are speaking "affirmations" to yourself already! In fact, all of your inner words are affirming something about you. Journaling can be an opportunity to look at what you are saying to yourself and see if you are affirming something that you actually agree with and want to continue holding as true. Do these affirmations affirm the parts of yourself that you want to strengthen? Do they sound like your voice, the voice of a parent, caregiver, former lover, or society? Are they loving, or do you have some work to do in learning how to re-parent yourself?

You might choose to create a journal practice with the concepts of this book in some of the following ways:

1. Use each affirmation as a journal prompt. Write it down and then ask yourself a series of questions: What do I notice when I say this affirmation to myself? Does it bring up any thoughts or feelings? If so, write them down.

2. Journal your way through a body scan. For example, when you say one of these affirmations to yourself, what do you feel in your body? Start at your feet and work your way up through each body part, area, or energy center. You will become more aware of your body as well as your energy through this practice. Be careful not to skip any body parts. If you do feel an aversion to checking in with certain parts of your body, write about it! This is not a bad thing but rather a gold mine of information. You will find as much of a way into yourself through the places in your body, mind, and life that you try to avoid as you'll find in those that you jump into with ease.
3. Free write. Write a page or more nonstop and then read what you've written. You can write about something specific or nothing. Just focus on filling the page.
4. Create your own affirmations. As you become aware that you are speaking to yourself all of the time, you will naturally begin to choose your words more carefully. Putting pen to paper is a way to engage with new ideas in a way that speaking alone can't quite do. Try writing some of the new things you'd like to believe about yourself, even if they don't feel true yet.
5. Keep a daily log of your process. What is it like for you to be taking on such a big, beautiful task as transforming your inner voice? As your inner voice shifts to become your greatest ally, you'll go through lots of ups and downs. Journaling can be

> a great way to see all of these "goods" and "bads" as simply neutral. In hindsight, even just looking back a week or two at a time, you'll see how something that felt like a bad thing turned out to be a valuable part of your growth.

HOW WE TALK TO OURSELVES MATTERS. We create our reality based upon our inner voice: a series of thoughts and beliefs that we agree with. When this agreement changes, our story changes and our life changes too. Affirmations introduce new truths to our subconscious so that we may create in alignment with what is true for the version of ourselves that is healed and thriving. In this way, we bring ourselves into experiencing that version of self.

BE GENTLE WITH YOURSELF THROUGH THIS PROCESS. As with any positive change, the old comes up to say goodbye on its way out! You may notice old beliefs, thought patterns, voices from your past, fears, and more coming to the surface. Keep in mind that you are seeing them because they are leaving. Wish them a fond farewell by thanking them for their service. They have attempted to keep you safe and supported. They have attempted to keep your identity intact. Let them know that they are now free to go. This process may be drastic to you, or it may be slow and subtle. Oftentimes the pains that have been yelling for our attention require more time and space to tell their stories than some of our whispers do. Give space to whatever comes up for you and use these affirmations as boundaries to hold a spacious channel open for your experience. You are safe and ready to go through this transformation.

ACCEPT WHAT COMES UP. The most important thing that you can do is be present with yourself. Being present is saying yes to yourself. Being present is self-acceptance. When we are honest about what's here, we have the power to alchemize it. If instead we attempt to reject any aspect of our experience, it will find another way to get our attention. This is where we see symptoms of dis-ease in the mental, emotional, and physical aspects of our being. The healing energy that is available to you in the present moment can absolutely transform your life, but the only way you give yourself access to it is to be present. I'll teach you.

AFFIRMATIONS ARE NOT JUST POSITIVE STATEMENTS. They are what is true when we strip away the beliefs that have clouded our vision of Self. When brought to the light of present-moment awareness, we begin to see that most of these beliefs are serving a version of us that doesn't even exist anymore. When our identity begins to shift, we start to shake off a lot of the outdated programs that kept us safe from long-ago threats. Use the affirmations in this book to challenge your currently held view of who you are and to reorient yourself to a perspective that is clear, spacious, and supports your growth.

RESTORE THE INNER VOICE. In time, you will create your own affirmations that come from your deepest desires for yourself and your life. They will be directed at your own pain, blind spots, and the things you desire to grow beyond or overcome. They will be celebrations of how far you've traveled and calls to action as you remember your power to choose which thoughts and beliefs you give your precious energy to. Your inner voice is within you and fully operational; there is nothing about it or you that is broken. As you do this work, you will remember that your symptoms, fears, addictions, and false beliefs are your tools to restore the clarity that will allow you to hear and take ownership of your inner voice. Throughout the course of this book, you will learn how to take your average day, your patterned responses, your thoughts, and your emotions and tune them to higher states of consciousness.

THE LIMITATIONS OF WORDS. As I'm sure you have noticed, this book is made out of words. I personally love words. I love the way words help ideas travel. But we would be doing ourselves a great disservice if we didn't also speak to the fact that words are also limiting. Words are a vehicle that transfers energy as well as a tool that initiates energetic alchemy. Each of these affirmations is designed as a cue to shift your energy. It is your work to notice how these affirmations feel to you emotionally as you work with them over time. You may find yourself meeting an affirmation differently each time you speak it to yourself. The limitation and the beauty of these affirmations is that they aren't exclusively true. For example, both "I know" and "I don't know" are true. It would be accurate to say that "I am perfect" and "I am imperfect." Throughout the course of this book, you will be learning to hold multiple truths at the same time even when it seems like they do not agree. This is one of the most valuable life tools that I have learned through my healing process thus far, and I am grateful to be sharing it with you.

THE PROTOCOL

You may use this protocol with each affirmation.

First, **GET IN TOUCH WITH WHAT IS.** Ask, What is true for me in this moment? How am I experiencing this truth? What do I notice about my thoughts, feelings, and sensations? Be honest with yourself. We liberate the energy needed for change by accepting what is presently operating within our consciousness.

Next, **CULTIVATE ACCEPTANCE.** Your experience is real. Simply being present with yourself is a profoundly healing act of self-love. Choose this. You deserve to have someone with you through the hard stuff; be that person.

Last, **INTRODUCE CHANGE.** Each affirmation invites you to change what is true for you. Your intention, the guiding principle of this work, need only be to see what changes within you as you go. The change will happen on its own through the magic of your presence. All you need to do is stay with yourself and you'll see how each thought, emotion, and sensation you experience transforms into a higher expression of itself.

THIS IS GRIEF WORK

You will find it helpful to continually reintroduce new concepts to the subconscious until they become integrated. You will know they are integrated when you no longer meet them at the level of fear. Fear arises when we offer change to our inner world because the change asks our identity to shift. In order for this new belief to be true, the version of you that believed something else must die. Therefore, this work involves grief. It will benefit you to support yourself through this process as if you were grieving the death of someone you love because you are going to learn to love yourself a whole lot, and you will surely change so much that the version of you who is reading this will become something of the past. At first, it will feel safer to stay the same, and you may find yourself repeating old habits, patterns, and addictions to certain thoughts that used to feel safe. However, the event that created a need for this effort to achieve safety is no longer happening, and you are now learning to create safety from a pure source. The version of you that exists in the future where you are happy, healthy, and fulfilled does not need the same protections that previous versions of you needed. You may now enter a new era of experimentation fueled by a brave curiosity to discover who you truly are. I promise you this: You will become who you tell yourself you are. It's time to change your story.

EXPRESSION TO INTEGRATION

As we do this work, old stories will rise to the surface, entering your awareness and asking for acceptance. Healing occurs when we offer these stories a space to speak through expression. Expression allows for release, and then integration occurs. Integration is the part of the process when whatever was previously painful to us transforms into a powerful gift that we are able to share with others. This work will teach you to alchemize what plagues you into the medicine that you have to share with the world. Different moments call for different means of expression. There may be times when you choose to journal, sing, dance, or paint, but oftentimes, you'll be in the midst of your day when you're using these affirmations. You'll find out what expression looks like for you in myriad contexts as you move through this work.

THE MANY VERSIONS OF THE SELF

You have permission to give every part of yourself a voice throughout this practice. You've written a million stories of who you are, and each was written from a different perspective in time. I like to think of this as having a million voices. They all sing together to create the version of me that I am now. When I am writing in my own journal, I make a special space for myself. I give permission to every voice to sing. This means that I may have one journal entry that says "I hate cheese" and another that says a love poem to Gouda. It doesn't matter that these things don't agree.

The work that you do for yourself is truly for you to experience yourself through the reflection you create when you express, whether that be in writing, an interaction with another person, or the words you say within your own mind.

AN UNDERSTANDING OF THE SUBCONSCIOUS MIND

The subconscious is like a library to which we hold an unlimited access card. We can visit at any time, day or night, and check out whatever books we like. There are some books we check out often, some we don't even know are there, and some we checked out ages ago that are long overdue to be returned.

We walk around carrying a backpack full of these books. The books in the backpack are the stories that create the beliefs we are operating with on a daily basis. Maybe we know what's in there; maybe we don't. How long has it been since you've looked in the backpack?

The backpack gets heavy and the shoulders tire while building up the strength to handle the immense responsibility of carrying so many books. Tension grows, headaches come, the body's balance is thrown off. New books join the backpack to try to remedy the problem, but their weight only makes things worse. What is the solution?

The solution is a trip to the library. We have to return some books!

So, how do we get to the library? There is but one door to the library, and it is the present moment. In order to access deeper aspects of the Self, we must simply arrive where we are, bringing our conscious awareness into focus and letting all parts of our experience be. Our access to the library expands as we go, and with practice, we can even read multiple books at a time, observing how they are all linked together. After all, they are all written by the same author!

Then, we take off the backpack. We cultivate a connection to self that is clean, clear, and powerful enough to support our exploration of its contents. This happens naturally as we return again and again to the library. As we get comfortable among the shelves and the smell of musty pages, we find ourselves setting the backpack down.

Next, we look inside. We've spent some time preparing for this moment. The excitement is palpable, the curiosity is childlike, and we are ripe with readiness! One by one, and often in series, we remove the books and peer inside, exploring the rich stories, the heartbreak, the joy, the challenge. We meet all of the characters who have been living within us: the hero, the martyr, the victim, the child. One by one, as we read each story, sometimes once and sometimes many times, we return each book to its rightful place on the shelf.

As the backpack becomes lighter, we begin to form a new sense of self. No longer do we see ourselves as heavy, slow, and limited by the weight of what we thought we must carry. Now, we know where to find each of our stories. We understand that we have unlimited access to each of them. We know how to get to the library, and we no longer have to carry anything with us at all times.

Now, we are free to form a new self-image, one which is no longer based on the stories of our past. Now, our stories fuel our passions and inspire our actions. Each new experience calls forth new aspects of self to be explored. Each expression of self creates new relationships with the world around us, and we watch it change to meet the new declaration of who we are. It is here that we find our truest self, our fulfillment, our dreams, and the energy to mobilize them.

ENERGY

Everything is energy, and energy is always moving. When we try to hold something steady, like a belief, it requires energy. What would happen if we let go so the mental energy could move naturally? Would we lose control, or would we gain a much higher form of control, where the innate ability of a living organism to reorganize to harmony naturally takes place?

The mind and heart are a team, as are all other aspects of the body and being. When the mind is holding energy rather than allowing it to pass through, we find ourselves stuck, unfulfilled, and unable to create. The artist might call it a block; sometimes we call it anxiety. For the purpose of this work, we can call it a pattern.

Mental energy moves the world around us. It is a mobilizing force that is both causal and receptive. As mental energy flows into the mind, we receive inspiration and new ideas. As it flows out of the mind, we communicate our thoughts with the world around us through our actions.

So, what happens when the mental energy is stuck in the same pattern? New, inspired thought is not able to enter the mind. Instead, we behave as we always have because we think how we've always thought, and thus, we experience what we've always experienced.

If, let's say, we are outwardly focused on the world outside of the library, we see evidence that reinforces our sense of self. It shows us that we ought to keep carrying the books we are carrying because those are the ones that we keep needing. It is not until we liberate the mental energy that the outer world begins to reflect a new identity.

Sure, we can create change in the outer world without ever visiting the library, but we will find that the changes made are still in accordance with our deeply held beliefs about the world and how we fit into it.

IDENTITY

It's the "me" and "them" mentality. Except, in this case, it's more like "me" and "not me." As young children, we begin to learn what we are and what we are not. The budding identity of a baby can be seen as they discover their separation from their mother. Soon, they are no longer experiencing life as a pure witness but rather will begin to experience themselves experiencing. By adulthood, this filter through which we view our experience, or sense of self, is well formed, and we expend immense energy in trying to keep it intact. We are well aware of what we are and what we are not, and the distinction is important so we don't get lost.

However, we may not realize that there is more flexibility in the lines we draw than we have come to believe. I am me; I am not my computer. I am me; I am not my cat. I am me; I am not the apple in my hand … Or am I?

Consider this: I know that the apple is not me, yet as soon as I eat it, it is. It seems, then, that the only difference between what I am and what I am not, in this case, is the time between me holding the apple and eating the apple. We might say that the apple became us instead of saying that we became the apple, but in truth, these two things became one. When we apply the same concept to identity, we see that the only difference between who we are now and who we are becoming is time. So, what if instead of projecting a past version of ourselves into the future via our thoughts and becoming that, we pause, we find the present moment, we remember our power to choose, and we choose to envision a future version of ourselves that feels empowered? Now, as with the apple, these two become one. This practice creates powerful changes in our identity and liberates us from past beliefs about ourselves that no longer serve us.

What if that future version of ourselves actually exists just because we imagined them? What if they have just as much power to create our present and past selves as we have to create them? What changes when our imagination becomes empowered? What if the cause and effect of our creation process can go both directions? What if we can actually create backward?

What we consume becomes us, which is the same as saying what we consume, we become. So, what if we start to consume some new thoughts, new stories, and new beliefs about who we are becoming? What changes in our lives if we give purpose to our past by thanking it for allowing us to become the future version of self that is happy, healthy, and empowered? How do we navigate the present moment when we are rooted in an inner voice that speaks to us lovingly and confidently?

YOU'RE NOT A FREQUENCY; YOU'RE A SYMPHONY

We can think of the human experience like a great symphony, more magnificent than any music on Earth, with millions of instruments, billions of tones, and trillions of varieties of timbre, which are all intelligent, intricately layered, and in motion. This divine dance of frequencies creates everything we know—from the apple to the sensual experience of it to the thoughts that arise while we're eating it. Every single aspect of our lives is a part of this energetic orchestra. When one instrument is out of tune, the whole song sounds off. The natural tendency of the symphony is to reorient to harmony, just as the natural tendency of life is to reorient to health and well-being.

Regardless of circumstances, we create our inner world, meaning that we create the experience of our circumstances. Only we decide which books we carry and which books are in the library. We are the librarian, the author, the reader, and the doorway into the room whose walls are lined with our stories. We alone hold the filter through which the external becomes internalized. It is our responsibility to choose how we experience our own lives. Herein lies our power.

It's not about the other; it's about the experience of the self in relationship to the other. This applies to any kind of other, whether the other be your home, spouse, career, government, a situation, or even a thought. We can't change others; we don't work from the place that they occupy. We work from where we are. We have the power to affect our inner world, and in doing so, we pull the strings on a level of creative functioning that precedes otherness. We work in the space that comes before the "me" and "not me." We change the truths we hold, and in doing so, the "other" responds. Shifts within demand shifts without. You have the power to change not just your world but the world around you by changing the world within you.

WHERE THOUGHT MEETS EMOTION

We categorize our emotional experience based on the way we perceive it. We have names for feelings: "sadness," "happiness," etc. When one feeling is far enough away on the spectrum from another, we consider them to be separate. However, they are not distinct entities. The space between emotions is not space at all but rather infinitely divisible information. And in the same way our ears are tuned to perceive a portion of the spectrum of sound, we are tuned to perceive a portion of the spectrum of emotion.

Emotion does not belong to those who can perceive it. In actuality, it is a part of the unified field of energy and exists as a spectrum of frequencies that make up our experience and extend beyond it. As humans, we perceive emotion through feeling. All life-forms experience emotion differently. Whether animal, mineral, plant, fungus, or molecule of water, we are all tuned in to the emotional layer of reality and equipped with unique mechanisms of experiencing it.

We do not generate emotion. It does not come from our bodies or minds. It does not come from our brains, which are a part of our bodies. Emotion simply exists, and we tap into it using the body and mind as tools. When we feel an emotion, we are experiencing a portion of the emotional spectrum as belonging to us or being our own. This happens because the frequency of the emotion resonates with that of our thoughts, or mental energy. We then identify with our emotional experience, saying, "This is me." A common way to express our emotions is with a statement like, "I am sad." A helpful alternative that is also more accurate is to say, "I feel sadness." Shifting this statement gives us the space to feel the emotion and observe it within us without becoming it. This creates the distance we need for emotions to shift, which liberates us from emotional patterns before they create havoc in our bodies, thoughts, and life circumstances.

As we learn to observe ourselves, we tune in to more subtle expressions of energy, including thoughts and emotions. We fine-tune our bodies as our intuitive instruments and learn to increase our capacity to both receive and express more.

HOW TO INTERACT WITH EMOTIONS

We can't choose our emotions by giving or withholding our energy like we can with thoughts. The way to interact with emotions is simply to feel them. When we give ourselves full permission to feel, the emotion transforms on its own and becomes a higher-octave version of itself. As a musician who has studied sound both in university as well as through a lifetime of music creation, I like to relate emotions to sound in order to better understand how they work. The musical alphabet gives letter names to tones: A, B, C, D, E, F, G, and then repeats infinitely. Each group of letters A through G is called an *octave*. These tones can also be represented by numbering their positions 1–7. This is just one system of many that breaks down the part of the spectrum of sound that we can hear into labeled tones so that we can identify them.

Musicians understand how to build chords, which are groups of tones, based on identifying the relationship between tones. For example, in the chord we call G major, the notes or tones played are 1, 3, and 5, which correlate to the letter names G, B and D, and are all played at the same time. Our ear recognizes the relationship between these tones as having a certain emotional feel to it. Major chords are typically felt as happy, while minor chords feel sad. Emotions work like notes in a chord, creating unique emotional or energetic flavors of feeling that we then associate with different people, places, situations, or times in our lives. Have you ever smelled the rain and felt the exact emotional flavor of a memory? Or maybe you've passed by a perfume that set in motion a cascade of emotional tones reminding you of the person you used to know who wore it? Emotions are complex. Even if they go by the same name, they won't feel the same every time we experience them. They will also feel different from one person to the next. Each emotional experience has tones as well as overtones, subharmonics, and movement.

EMOTIONAL OCTAVES

Just like in music where every note can be repeated in infinitely higher and infinitely lower octaves, or groups of tones, each emotion also has an expression of itself that is higher or lower in frequency, and we can perceive this through how an emotion feels. For example, the higher octave of jealousy is appreciation. Both occur when we identify something as being valuable to us, but one is based in the fear of loss while the other comes from a space of trust and abundance. When we notice which of our emotions and thoughts are paired together, we can see how they energetically feed each other. We can make it a practice to notice what jealousy feels like in our bodies. Our heart rate may increase, our throat may feel tight, and our palms may perspire. If we get familiar with the feeling of this, or any other emotion, it can trigger us to check in with our thoughts. After noticing the physical sensations of an emotion, we can approach our mind as a curious observer. We might find that our jealousy is paired with a thought such as losing something we love, not being enough, or missing an opportunity that matters to us. Recognizing our emotions helps us to learn which of our thoughts are benefiting us and which we can let go of in order to function in more harmony with nature and our deeper sense of self. This practice also shows us what holds importance to us, enlightening us to our passions while giving us an opportunity to approach these things from a place of empowerment rather than fear.

RIDING THE WAVES

With practice and a dedication to observing how we work, we start to recognize patterns and find opportunities to make changes to them. Soon, you'll see how one emotion transforms into the next. We don't jump from one emotional state to another but rather ride an emotional wave through a landscape of information, temporarily arriving at something that is both new and familiar. What makes an emotional state feel new isn't that it has just been discovered by us for the first time but rather that new thoughts are happening in tandem with it. When our point of perspective is far enough away from any other part of our experience, we see the other part as being not a part of us. So, we may say, "Now I am happy; sadness is not a part of my experience right now." Still, that sadness is accessible to us, and we may return to it. It still belongs to us, and it is still a part of the full spectrum of emotion that we are tapped into at all times.

FEELING

When we feel our emotions, they naturally move and transform within us. Feeling emotions prevents them from getting sticky, hanging around longer than we need them, or trying to get our attention in other ways. When we accept what we are feeling, our emotions ascend to higher vibrations, and our thoughts ascend to higher, more open, receptive, and creative states of consciousness. When we notice ourselves feeling a lower-octave emotion—for example, worry or fear—we can pay attention to the thought that accompanies it and accept the pair without assigning them any meaning. This allows our thoughts and emotions to unbind and shift. From here, we can offer ourselves a new thought that feels just a little bit more supportive. For example, "I won't be able to pay the rent on time if I have to spend all my money on this car repair" is quite a fear-inducing thought. We could move gently into a higher emotional state by offering a new thought like "I'm not sure how I will be able to pay the rent if I have to spend a lot of my money on this" and then "What if I do find a way to pay the rent despite this unforeseen expense?" and then "I trust that I'll be okay, even if I am not sure how this will work out yet. I am resourceful, and I believe in my ability to be creative and solve problems." Or we can simply state, "Things are always working out for me."

When we find the courage to stay present with our experience, no matter what thoughts and emotions arise, we naturally spiral upward, increasing our capacity to be with our experience. This means we create less moments of trauma, that which cannot be felt or integrated in the moment it occurs, and more moments of meaning, peace, and ease.

EMOTION IS THE MOBILIZING FORCE OF CREATION

No thing is ultimately separate from any other. All things are touching. All parts are interacting aspects of the same, generative whole. Consider light and sound. They behave very differently, but both exist as expressions of the unified field of energy that everything is a part of. Thought and emotion are much the same. Thought exists in what we call the mental plane while emotion hangs out nearby, functioning so much differently that we would say it has its own spectrum. But all the while, both are expressions of the energetic whole. Thought and emotion work together, magnetizing each other. And they need each other. Without emotion, we would not perceive thought. Think of each thought like a 2D image on a roll of film and emotion like the light that shines through it, allowing the image to be projected and perceived. Emotion gives us the ability to perceive our thoughts.

Without emotion, our mental energy would have no creative force. You may say, "But I have lots of thoughts that don't feel like anything at all!" Throughout the work you're embarking on with this book as your guide, you'll find yourself tuning in to subtleties of both thought and emotion. You'll begin to be able to feel the emotional energy that accompanies even the most insignificant, minute thoughts. The most exciting part, in my opinion, is when you begin to notice the emotion, or energy, attached to each of your words. From here, you get to start purposefully choosing to speak the energy into the world that you want to create.

PATTERNED THINKING

Without present-moment awareness, our default is to tune ourselves to experience the emotion that is closest to that which was attached to similar thoughts in the past. This is the recipe for our mental patterning, which creates our patterned life experience. So, which came first, the thought or the emotion? There is no starting or ending place; thought and emotion are simultaneous but not inseparable. Our power reveals itself when we deliberately choose to feel a specific frequency range of the emotional spectrum by thinking a particular thought that stimulates it.

The moment that we notice we are thinking is an opportunity to interrupt patterned thought and emotion. If a thought arises that feels unsafe, negative, or fearful, we simply replace it with a thought that feels even slightly more supportive of a calm, confident self. For example, if we notice ourselves thinking something unsupportive like "Bad things always happen to me," we can introduce a new thought like "This has happened to me before, and I am curious to explore this pattern." And then, maybe, "What would change in my life if I stopped expecting bad things to happen as my default?" Now, we have disconnected from the initial disempowered emotional state by introducing and beginning to follow curiosity in a new direction. We've made space to do an experiment and can introduce a new statement by stating something like "Bad things only happen sometimes. Sometimes good things happen." Maybe the next time we notice this pattern we have made enough space to move straight from "Bad things always happen to me" to "Everything is always happening for me, even if I can't always see how it benefits me right away."

Through this process, we've changed the thoughts, but more importantly, we've changed the emotional state or "frequency" that we are experiencing. This then allows us to naturally attract more good-feeling thoughts and feel more good-feeling emotions, creating an empowered version of self. This also tunes our awareness to find evidence to support our new statement rather than the old one. So, we will start to see our new beliefs affirmed in our lives and, therefore, create a new experience for ourselves that is more supportive. Soon, we begin to notice everything that is working out for us and how the things we may have, in the past, initially judged as "bad" were opportunities for learning and growth. Our actions align with how we view ourselves and the world around us, so now, we can go forward creating from an inner state that supports building more of the experiences we want to have.

INTENTION

We have our ultimate intention—that of being and experiencing our true self as love. Then, we have life experiences that create disassociation from the core truth of our being. When this happens, we create patterns of thought and emotion that seek to return us to experiencing ourselves as the awareness of our true self. In other words, there isn't love and not-love. There is awareness of love and the absence of that awareness. In the absence of that awareness, we experience the intention of redirection that guides us back to experiencing the awareness of love once more. When we experience this process beyond the lived illusion of time, we see love. Only love. In truth, love is all there is. When we expand beyond the experience of time, we see how nothing is separated except by time. Which means, of course, that nothing is separate at all. Yet, our experience of separation is simultaneously real. Again, we're learning to hold multiple truths.

We can choose to mobilize a thought on a new emotional intention, one that resonates in harmony with our most basic frequency of love.

When we tune ourselves to love, we transcend the emotional experience and become the truth of who we are, the whole being that can experience any range of thought or emotion without identifying with it. Love destroys our beloved illusion. Remembering ourselves as love liberates our creative energy and returns us to living in the flow state of conscious creation. You are love expanding in infinite expression, viewing itself, believing itself. If life is a dream, then love is the dreamer. You are the dream, and you are the dreamer.

It's time to remember the inner path, where every moment of your life becomes an opportunity, every circumstance is your medicine, and every word is a channel to receive.

PART 2
Affirmations

A reminder, you don't have to agree with these affirmations in order to use them. Use each affirmation as an invitation to approach your inner world with curiosity. Say yes to whatever comes up, treat it as your perfect starting point for change, and go from there.

I Can Choose

We can choose our thoughts. Our thoughts are the tools we need to change our world. Both your personal world and the world we all share are directed by our mental energy. Many of us have experienced our thoughts as a place of struggle, perhaps even associating the term *mental health* with its opposite: *mental unwellness*. It is time to reveal the truth. Our thoughts are a place of great opportunity.

You might believe that you are not able to choose your thoughts. This is a belief that most of us have grown up with because no one modeled how to do this. As caregivers typically focus on behavior and not the thoughts that precede it, this essential skill is simply not something we're taught. The good news is, the opportunity to change your relationship with your mind never goes away. Now, I will show you how to retrain your mind to become your most powerful ally in creating the life of your dreams.

We are all remembering our power. There will be many ways and many teachers as we collectively wake up to more and more of what has previously been subconscious. The patterns that have been chosen for us are brought to our awareness and liberated through this work. As we uncover them, we are presented with the opportunity to take responsibility for our lives, our thoughts, and how we direct our energy. Through this process of learning to consciously choose which thoughts deserve our attention, we free ourselves from being a victim to emotional states, moods, or patterned thinking.

I invite you to use the affirmation "I can choose" as a reminder that you are an incredibly powerful, creative being who is equipped with the mental tools to build worlds. You can use this power at any time simply by choosing to. And if you don't believe you have the power to choose, you can start now with retraining that thought process by using this affirmation.

Throughout this book, you will be presented with many opportunities to choose. You can choose to allow these new ways of thinking into your internal landscape or reject them. I encourage you to let them in, trusting that your own awareness and inner compass are powerful enough to tell you what deserves to stay. You'll find that many things reorganize. You'll let go of the beliefs that no longer make sense when new, larger truths are introduced. You'll cultivate an inward-facing awareness that allows you to make the cuts with precision and accuracy. You'll find your power to choose.

We choose our thoughts by directing our energy. Your energy is your attention. Every moment presents the opportunity to first see what is being thought and then to choose whether or not to feed that thought.

Just like feeding a fire, when there is something for the fire to eat, it grows larger. It spreads. When there is nothing to burn, or no oxygen, the fire goes out. Your thoughts will grow when you feed them your attention. Some of your thoughts have been fed so much and for so long that they have become beliefs—the thoughts you don't realize you can change.

Thoughts and beliefs only require the light of your awareness in order to change. They don't need you to know how to change them. They don't need you to organize them or even to know how to let them go. The awareness itself is what sets a thought free so that it may reorganize itself based on the loving intention you have to see yourself flourish. Awareness is acceptance of what is. And acceptance is a most loving choice. This is all the love that is needed in order for you to gain control over your thoughts. Awareness puts love in control, and love will do beautiful things with your mind.

First, choose awareness. Then, choose love. If a thought feels loving, keep it. Feed it; think it again. If a thought feels harmful, let it go by either choosing a more loving thought or by starving it. Either way, you'll see it crumble in the presence of love as a new and inspired thought naturally arises to take its place.

At first, this process may feel clunky and unnatural. But over time and with dedicated practice at choosing to be aware of what you are thinking and feeling, you will come into a position of mastery, instantly knowing which thoughts are beneficial to you and the world around you. You'll know because you'll recognize the feeling of each thought, and you'll be able to assess it immediately without having to think about it at all. You will learn to break the cycle of anxious or repetitive thinking. You will stop thinking about your thoughts. This book will help you restore your inner compass so that you may feel adeptly and then make soul-led choices.

It Is Safe to Be Alone

It is aloneness that allows for togetherness, individuality that allows for community, and stillness that allows for movement. We all share the innate desire for connection, with ourselves, with other people, with nonhuman creatures, with our planet, and with energies that are beyond our current scope of awareness. It is this intention for connection that guides us through our lives. When we are aware of this intention, we can consciously participate in the process of creating connections that nourish, support, and sustain us. I invite you to use the affirmation "It is safe to be alone" to remind yourself that you are a safe person to be alone with and to thus strengthen your ability to be with others as well.

Oftentimes, we avoid being alone with ourselves because we perceive ourselves as a threat to our own safety and well-being. We might choose to consume information, media, food, or substances to keep a distance from our own thoughts and feelings. We might even consume other people in the sense that we use their company to fill space that would otherwise allow aspects of our own experience to rise to our awareness.

When we recognize what we are consuming, or what we are using to fill the space in our lives, we can begin to release those things and relax into the fullness of our experience.

The foundation of this process is a fundamental truth: Our thoughts and feelings cannot hurt us. It is what we do with our thoughts and feelings that can hurt or help us. In order to experience our thoughts and feelings in a way that supports and nourishes us rather than hurts us, we must release our attempt to control them. This means we need to feel all of our emotions. We can use mindful awareness to observe our thoughts without reacting to them or organizing them. To do this, we must think and feel without identifying as the thought or emotion. Life is less scary when your idea of who you are doesn't change every time you think or feel something different.

We are working within an interconnected web of thoughts and feelings. It is the awareness of the relationship between our thoughts and feelings that frees us from our past. We can call this forgiveness, integration, or acceptance. Finding ourselves where we are now is always a helpful tool to get an accurate look at why and how we are choosing to connect with ourselves, others, and the placeholders that provide an illusion of safety.

The past is no longer happening, but our past mental and emotional experiences create the filter through which we view the present moment. Thoughts are mental energy and exist in their own plane of reality that we all have access to. We quite literally attract them into our awareness. The creation process is such that our thoughts precede our actions.

Even in moments of pure reactivity, we are choosing action based on structures of experience and belief that exist within us as mental energy, or thoughtform. Expanding our awareness gives us the opportunity to perceive and direct mental energy with our intention. This is how we consciously create our lives and the world around us.

We can choose to direct our mental energy with the intention of creating love, balance, peace, ease, prosperity, and freedom. When we choose this, the natural result is healthy connection between all aspects of ourselves and between ourselves and other people.

Our emotions are the compass within us that shows us which intention we are using to direct the creation of our lives. When we feel tightness, fear, and dis-ease, we are being shown that we are holding our mental energy tightly in stagnation. To release our mental energy and free up our process of creation so that we might see aspects of our lives change, we must feel everything that is present as it arises. When we do this, we are guiding our lives with love. Our willingness to fully feel is true self-acceptance because it is us saying yes to what is real and present in the moment. This allowance of "what is" shifts our mental energy and shows up as changes in our bodies, life circumstances, and environments because it is connected to the mental energy that precedes the creation of each of these things.

This is self-love. We release our control on one level to gain control on a higher level and direct our lives with the intention that takes care of all of the details for us. All we need to do is feel completely, think openly, and express ourselves to connect with others throughout the process. There is no wrong way to feel and no wrong thought to think. When we allow our thoughts and feelings to exist in us, we are validating them. Acceptance is what gives them the space to transform, or heal. Acceptance allows us to notice patterns and find means of expression and support.

To fully connect with others, we must connect within. To connect within, we must feel safe when we are alone, or focused inward. We don't have to wait to connect with others until after we do this inner work; it's not one before the other. This work of connection within can happen anytime we choose to bring our awareness to our inner experience. We do not have to wait to share our process until we have it all figured out. We simply need to be present with ourselves as we go, accepting ourselves as living, growing beings. The true meaning of forgiveness is to give ourselves the space to feel and think without judgment, and it liberates all stuck energy.

Release your expectations of what your process should look like and simply continue to try. You will fine-tune, restoring your ability to hear your inner wisdom as you go. You will begin to see that structures, whether in your personal life or collectively, that do not match your intention of love will naturally fall. Use the affirmation "It is safe to be alone" to remind yourself that your thoughts and feelings are safe and that in experiencing them you are choosing love, which creates healing beyond your wildest dreams. Your aloneness is safe and will help your connections flourish.

I Am Listening; I Am Heard

When we speak, we are always heard and always received by the part of us who is always listening. When we want to be heard, we must start with hearing ourselves.

There is an energy within each of us that animates our bodies, inspires our actions, and magnetizes thoughts into the space that is our "mind." This is the energy of Life itself. That's Life with the big "L," the higher power we can all agree on. Life expresses completely uniquely in each of us, and because of that, we are each gifted the opportunity to create something no one else can create. Even in the moments we are simply being, we are creating an experience, our experience. I invite you to use the affirmation "I am listening; I am heard" to free any and all blocks that you have to creating freely.

Your mind is an open space, a prairie field where many thoughts have grown and burned, where some roots remain deeply hidden. Here, some flowers show their colors, while others patiently await their divinely timed bloom. It is here, among the brambles, that we begin to notice the relationships between each stone, stalk of mullein, and wild rose. Here, we tune ourselves in to the subtle buzz of a delicate visitor and listen for the wind as its song plays through a million blades of grass. If we spend enough time here, we begin to notice everything: We see how the colors pair in contrasts, the yellow and purple, red and green. We feel how long it takes a petal to fall. We notice not just what's alive here but how it moves. It is here that we begin to observe our patterns. Here, the relationship between our thoughts and emotions becomes clear.

Our voice is not just the sound that we express outwardly. We have an inner voice as well. The inner voice takes the form of thought and plays intimately with our emotions. No matter if our words are spoken internally or externally, there is an aspect of us that is always listening. When we choose to bring the voice within into the light of our awareness, we fulfill our deep desire to be heard. The practice of listening is all we need to clear away unnecessary noise and restore our ability to hear ourselves.

Awareness functions as a feedback loop. We say something, and awareness returns it back to us so we may hear our own voice. We watch as our words and tone manifest into thoughts, emotions, and circumstances, telling us about our experience, our desires, and our met and unmet needs. When we hear ourselves, we empower ourselves to create the circumstances through which others can hear us as well. We magnetize others to our voice. Your voice matters. In fact, it is needed. Your voice is powerful enough to create change both within you and outside of you.

To be heard is to be accepted for who we truly are, and to be accepted is to be loved. Choosing to listen to ourselves means listening not just to our thoughts but also to the judgment that follows. We can choose to love the parts of ourselves that are thinking the thought, the parts that are judging the thought, and the past experiences that created them both. All we must do to love ourselves fully in the experience of each moment is be present. Feel, notice, listen. This choice of loving everything as it is, as it arises within us, creates a sense of inner safety that repatterns our mental and emotional landscape.

Love to the mind is like a fire to the prairie, burning thoughts to the ground, calling every belief into question. "Do you need to be here? Do you serve me?" Love asks. Love trusts the soil to hold on to what belongs while transforming everything that no longer resonates with its frequency. When we bring awareness to our inner world, we invite love to touch every thought. This requires a great amount of trust. From this space of trusting love to work on us and through us, we are able to cultivate a love for ourselves that mobilizes us toward opportunities to express our truth in more fullness, with more colors, textures, and tones.

When we are listening, we are able to receive the inspired direction of the life that lives us and take inspired action. From this state, we meet our questions with patience, curiosity, and wisdom. It is from the state of listening that our speech is guided by our inspiration. Tuned in to the depths of what is true for us, we speak that which carries truth, that which has meaning. This is our authentic voice.

While the world thirsts for authenticity, many of us are still afraid to speak. We carry the wound of not being heard. We fashion a belief that says our voice is not worthy. It can make us louder, begging for our need to be met, or quieter, as we fear being met with a response that is unsafe. In either case, our needs become demands rather than commands as we speak them with the expectation of being unheard.

Our wounds ask us to make a cruel transaction. They believe the lie that we can trade our authenticity for safety, while, in fact, our authentic expression is what creates safety. Even if the outward circumstances of our lives are not yet safe for us to speak freely, there is always the option to create a safe space within. As we begin to listen to ourselves, our true tone emerges once again, uninhibited by the debris of structures we once created in order to protect ourselves. We show ourselves that we are safe, and in doing so, we remember what safety feels like. Then, we can bring this intuition to our life circumstances, settling for nothing less.

No longer do the times that we were unsafe keep us caged. When we let our past limit our self-expression, we show ourselves and the world a limited version of who we are. In time, we start to believe it. But through listening, we bring the medicine that restores our truth. We don't need to identify the roots of the wound in order to heal it; we need simply be brave enough to let the fire of love do its work. We need simply be brave enough to listen.

Use the affirmation "I am listening; I am heard" to remind yourself that all of the tools you need are already within you. Listen and you will be heard not just by yourself but by the ones who are waiting to hear you.

My Voice Matters

We all know that our voice has a frequency because we hear it as sound. But did you know that your inner voice has a frequency too? We may not experience our inner dialogue sonically, but we do experience it as a part of the same field of energetic frequencies that sound, light, and all else ultimately belong to. I invite you to use the affirmation "My voice matters" to invite more of your own unique soul voice into your life. Observe as the voice within you directs the change within your world. You'll see that the words spoken silently are very much heard by every aspect of your being.

The way you talk to yourself matters. Straight up. It does. You can get away with being a jerk to yourself, sure. No one is coming to scold you. There is no punishment. However, there is a consequence to every action, and words, being energy in motion, are actions. If you want to change the way the world responds to you, you must change your inner voice—the stories you tell about who you are, what the world is, and what you expect.

You may find yourself echoing the voices of others, and you may, for a while, believe that these voices are your own. You may have adopted them a long time ago, even in childhood. You may have spoken like someone else for so long that you actually believe it is you. But as soon as you bring your attention to the voice within, something changes. You begin to be able to identify the voice of your soul and the lesser voices that merely attempt to speak to it. When you bring the light of your awareness to the way you are talking to yourself "in your own head," you start to navigate with your own heart.

Each word is an offering to the version of you that expects it. The child within you who was shown that the only way to learn was to be scolded receives the harshest words. The lover who believes the lies of a former partner stays trapped in a relational agreement that has long since passed. There is no need, no reason, to stay locked in to something that is no longer happening. But the mind doesn't let go of emotionally charged stories until awareness enters the picture. Your awareness frees your mind by allowing the thought and emotion to sever. Then, the thought exists and the emotion exists, but they live parallel, not intertwined. The web loosens as you claim your power to reweave it. The thought finds its place in the mind and the emotion finds its place in the heart. The heart is the only place that emotion can be processed. With the emotion free to be felt, the thought is now free to transform. This is where we see the inner voice change its tone. This is where we introduce the frequency of love back into our inner world so it becomes our way of being and infuses every moment of our creation with the love that we are. This is how we create the world we want to live in.

You are so creative that you can literally build a new life story for yourself, a new truth, simply by changing the words you attach to your past. There is a version of you that lives back there, and they are limited by the language of your thoughts in a past moment. But now, you have more options. You can design a fresh framework, a new way to see yourself, simply by choosing new words. Use the affirmation "My voice matters" to introduce a new truth, to restore your inner power to choose your words. Use these words, "My voice matters," as a declaration of self-love and self-respect and to reset your expectations for the treatment you'll accept from the voice within and the voices without.

I Am Creative

Consider that each of us is a tone made up of many millions of lesser tones that bind together to create the "shape" of our own unique sound. Consider too that this shape is alive, always changing, expanding, and folding, allowing us to experience its different harmonic resonances as the relationship continually shifts between the point of our awareness and the rest of our self. This shape is multidimensional, and therefore its behavior is challenging to categorize in ways that make sense to the mind. Luckily, we can make peace with these larger-than-life concepts through our creativity. It is here that we come to understand ourselves in ways that more closely mimic the patterns of the whole creative being that we are a part of.

When we begin to become aware of the beliefs that create our relationships with the world around us, we see the filter through which we are creating. Seeing it allows us to make intentional choices about the creation of the filter itself.

We've all seen it: An art gallery houses a twelve-by-twelve canvas with a single, giant paint splotch splayed across its center. It's red, just red. The onlookers stare, considering the esoteric meaning of such a piece. "What could the artist be saying?" they ask. A man sobs; a woman hides her face as tears stream down her cheeks, moved by the pure emotional energy of the blob. Then someone calls out, "This is art? My three-year-old could make this in like … five minutes!" And this summarizes everything.

One winter in my early twenties, I was working at a museum and feeling entirely unfulfilled by my job. I was pregnant with my first child and took the city bus twice per day between my home on the West Side to the frigid heart of St. Paul, Minnesota. The buildings towered high and blocked the sun, so even the not-so-cold days felt ten degrees colder. On this particular morning, the wind barreled down the tunnellike streets, a force that made walking even more difficult than it already was in a body learning to open. I could feel the power of nature both within me and outside of me asking me to slow down among the rush of the city. As I walked, deep in thought over who I was and who I was becoming, I looked down and noticed the ground before me was strewn with tiny yellow leaves. They surprised me, bold and bright against the gray of the concrete. Each one existed in stark contrast to the metal that climbed toward the matching silver sky, and they were just exactly the size and shape of cigarette butts. In fact, my first impression was that they were trash until I noticed their aliveness.

I was carried back into a memory of my work at a nearby music venue just blocks away: How I would sweep the patio clean at the end of each shift, exhausted and on the other side of midnight. How cold my hands were then. How angry I'd felt when I'd consider what a person must be thinking, or ignoring, to lay their trash on the belly of my mother. How angry I was that she'd been covered with concrete in the first place. My sweeping felt like a ritual then, something I did not just for the checklist on the far end of the bar but a sacred task to remind me that there was something bigger. That I was bigger than that little job, than the things the patrons said about me in passing, than the day, than the tips, than the version of me who swept.

So much meaning was evoked in the moment I saw the leaves. Such a simple sight. I watched as others passed, eyes to their phones or lost in thought as they walked. Maybe I was lost too, but in a way, I felt found. I had spent the last few years convincing myself I was an artist, and in the months since receiving my daughter in my womb, my identity was in the midst of such a deep transformation that I feared I'd have to let the title go. In fact, just days before I saw the leaves, my coworker had asked me to introduce myself to a new volunteer at the museum, and my words hit the floor: "I don't know who I am right now." But this, now, was somehow both new and ancient. It was inspiration. And I suddenly realized that it wasn't my way with words that made me a poet. It was the way I could see. It was the space I made within myself to feel. And I realized in that moment, and again in many more, that I was an artist not because of what I created but because of how I created.

So, maybe it's a big paint blob on a wall that costs ninety billion dollars and makes people cry, and maybe you think it's nuts. But maybe I'm nuts too for looking at a leaf and falling in love. Maybe your art looks crazy to other people or it doesn't look like art at all. Sometimes I create a meal, sometimes a song; sometimes I have to remind myself that in these times when motherhood requires 150 percent of my energy it's okay if all I create in a day is a childhood.

The thing is, we are creating all of the time, whether we realize it or not, whether we call it art or not. By making this process conscious, we open up a world of possibilities that, without the proper lens, the sleeping creative is unable to see. When one becomes awake to the true purpose of their life as a creator, everything shifts. The "how" we create changes drastically and reflects the true meaning of the "why." We begin to see ourselves differently, not as a sad symptom of a suffering world but rather as a blooming fractal of life reflecting infinite potential.

In the times when I thought things couldn't get any darker, I remembered this. My hope rode on the possibility that if we could all just realize that we have the power to create our inner experience of the world, and that our inner experience creates the world, the world would change. So, maybe it's not about doing it all, and maybe we're not running out of time. Maybe it's okay to be one little person in an infinite sea. Maybe the power of your uniqueness and mine is that we each get to contribute something that only we can. And maybe, just maybe, it feels pretty amazing to live with the understanding that our existence actually does mean something.

Use the affirmation "I am creative" to remind yourself to create on purpose. Even if your creations don't meet your expectations or someone else's, they are valuable because they are an expression of you, and you are valuable. Just keep creating. Continue to allow yourself to be inspired to make meaning, even in your darkest moments. Creating on purpose gives your life purpose. Be art.

I Accept Myself

Self-acceptance is the greatest act of self-love, because acceptance of anything is simply acknowledging that it exists. Acceptance is honest. If we're always trying to make ourselves fit into the version of us that we deem worthy of love, we're constantly missing the mark. We're missing the opportunity that is here, now, in every moment, to simply be the love that we are. We can set goals to become a version of ourselves that is even more alive, and we can lay the infrastructure within to meet them. But we don't have to believe the lie that says we must meet the goal before we are allowed to be loved.

Love is not a reward. It's a way of being. And it's a choice.

I invite you to use the affirmation "I accept myself" to remind yourself that you are worthy of love now, as is. There is no need to wait. The goal will be met either way, whether you love yourself to it or hate yourself to it. However, you'll have a much better time if you choose love. Not only does this choice reflect the true beauty of who you are and infuse your every action with its power, but it also simply feels much, much better.

To accept yourself is to say yes to the fullness of your experience. We no longer spend energy building boxes to lock parts of ourselves away: "This goes here; that goes there; this for later; that for never." The inner dialogue of a person in denial of their fullness is exhausting. When we assign the mind the job of the heart, it falls short. It tires. We expend immense amounts of our life force trying to keep things organized when, if we'd let go, things would naturally fall into place. When we say yes to ourselves, we remind ourselves that it is safe to feel. Then, the heart can do its job. This is the healing gift of self-acceptance. When you say yes to yourself, you tell yourself that it is safe to be you.

Meet yourself in each moment with open arms and you will transform. You'll bloom—just like a child with a loving caregiver or a flower with the attention of a gardener. In meeting yourself with self-acceptance, you take ownership of your environment. You nourish yourself and invite the change that needs to take place for your growth. This way of being will undoubtedly bring up the emotional memories of the times you were not met with such care. Luckily, the plan is the same for anything that comes up. Accept it by feeling it and acknowledging it fully, which sets it free, and then watch it change.

An added benefit of this work is that by accepting the challenge to treat yourself with unconditional love, you begin to understand how you should be treated by others. You may then choose to make choices that support your life. Just as the gardener may remove a pest from their beloved plant, you may choose to lovingly distance yourself from those who do not treat you with the love you now know as your new normal. That, or you will teach them a new way to treat you by the example you set. Additionally, you'll learn to accept others and save yourself immense energy that otherwise would be put toward trying to change them. There is a faster and more effective way to influence others, and it is to inspire them. Through self-acceptance, you position yourself to do just that. Your bravery is required for this process, as is your willingness to change, and I promise you, you will change.

My Body Is Safe

When I was in the beginning stages of my healing journey, my body was the last place I wanted to be, and yet, it was the first place I woke up each morning. I couldn't escape myself no matter how hard I tried to ignore the pain and fear woven through my tissues. It took my physical symptoms of dis-ease getting exceptionally loud for me to realize that tuning in to the subtle sensations and energetics of my experience was the only way through my trauma. At that point, although the trauma had ended and I was no longer in a threatening situation, my body wasn't convinced. Physically, I was living in the past. It was as if my body believed that I was an unsafe place to be.

Here we are at the feet of a tall juxtaposition. The body is only ever in the present, and yet, in cases like mine and many others' (both more and less extreme), the body behaves as if it is living in the past. How could this be? Wouldn't it stand to reason that the body should, of all things, be functioning purely free in the true limitlessness of the present moment? This was one of the big questions that set me on the path of embodiment.

I was diagnosed with PTSD (post-traumatic stress disorder) at age twenty-one, just after joining an eating disorder therapy program. At the time, the diagnosis felt like a life sentence. But I refused to believe that the rest of my life could be determined by someone else's choices. I had already freed myself of the diagnosis of OCD. Why couldn't I overcome this too? Call it hopelessly stubborn or hope itself, I was determined to live free—free of the label, but most importantly, free in my body, which I soon came to realize simply meant safe in my body.

Use the affirmation "My body is safe" to invite the fullness of your experience to exist within the vessel of your body. These words introduce a new model for experiences to filter through, a new pathway for information to flow, and a new structure through which meaning is derived. In other words, this affirmation helps you to create a belief that supports your health and well-being. When thoughts group together, they form beliefs, and it is our beliefs that tell emotion how to behave in our bodies. Bringing awareness to our beliefs restores full health not just to our bodies but to our minds and to our life circumstances. When you begin to bring attention to your body and listen with an open heart, you'll notice that physical sensations are attached to thoughts and emotions. There is no separation between any of these, and we can work on the level of any of them to affect the others.

You'll find your own ways of bringing awareness back to your body simply by operating with the intention of doing so. Use the affirmation "My body is safe" to affirm your intention to experience safety, wholeness, and completion within your own body. We don't need to have a special diet, lifestyle, or talent to do this work; we just need to have a body.

If you've been looking for something, it's surely in your body. Our bodies are doors into other realms. Two of those realms are thought and emotion. I like to think of emotion as the energy that runs through our bodies or the way that our bodies interpret energy. Our bodies hold not just the key to every door but every door. This includes pain. When we accept our pain and give it the freedom to move in us, it transforms into something new. We can receive the gifts we've asked for when we let our pain speak.

The body is the map to everything that is seemingly "outside" of what we identify with. Imagine asking a question but being terrified to hear the answer because it might threaten your sense of self, the very "I" that you believe yourself to be. If you believe that the answer to your prayers, the manifestation of your desire, or the answer to your question is going to hurt you, you will not hear the answer. Your body will block the door because your belief says that your identity needs to be protected. Here we see pain, tension, confusion, and dis-ease on the physical level of our being. We can receive the gifts we've asked for when we listen to our bodies with the willingness to allow our emotions to move however they need. We don't have to understand this process before we do it because the body, mind, and emotions are intelligent, and they inform us as we go.

What if each of us could feel the power in our physical form? What if each of us knew that no judgment, no assault or abuse, no thought or word could ever take away the freedom that rests in each cell of our bodies? This is the reality we create when we trust our bodies.

After enduring the abuse that I went through as a young adult, I thought something had been taken from me. I searched for it, desperately wanting to become whole again. At first, I thought I had to get it back from the person who stole it. Then, I thought it was something I could find if I went deeper within myself. Eventually, on this journey inward, I realized that nothing had ever been taken. Rather, I was given something that I never asked for. I was carrying layers of illusion that clouded my vision of who I truly was. The work wasn't to find something that was missing; it was to uncover what had become hidden beneath the pain, coping mechanisms, and patterned thinking that I adopted to survive the abuse.

When we experience trauma of any magnitude, the body has something to say about it and calls us toward expression in order to release and integrate our experience. Luckily, since we have a body in every moment, every moment is an opportunity to practice tuning in to the body. When we start to view symptoms as neutral information rather than judging them as being negative, we can begin the process of deeply listening to the body.

The body speaks to us through sensation, and as we tune in to what we can feel in our bodies, we learn to feel more. The senses sharpen and expand, allowing more information into our field of awareness. Eventually, the sensations become more than physical, and we develop another critical skill, which is the ability to sense nonphysical energy. However, because nonphysical energy exists more subtly than the physical sensations we are used to, we have to start with what is easiest to feel and allow the expansion to happen naturally.

The body also guides us in how to move in ways that naturally maintain and restore health. When we move intuitively, we build a bridge of trust between the mind and body, which restores right relationship and invites the body to continue to offer more guidance. The same is true with eating. When we listen to the thoughts and emotions that come up around food, we begin to weave a web of understanding how it all relates. We might find that a certain emotion is attached to a certain craving or that the anxiety of meal planning or grocery shopping shuts us down emotionally, making it harder to recognize the guidance of our internal compass in other areas of our lives. When we take the approach of exploring our inner world with curiosity, the outer world changes. This is because we are doing the work of connecting the dots. Dots love to be connected. They form pictures, blending our feelings with past experiences, liberating memories and tension in our tissues, and ultimately delivering us to a more present, clear self. Each of these affirmations teaches us the tools we need to be present with our experience and tune in to the body's complex relationship with our mind and emotions. This work is absolutely worth it.

No longer can we subscribe to the idea that the body is just a meat suit. The body is not optional. It is an instrument of our consciousness and a sacred door. The body is not just a vehicle for our consciousness to experience life on Earth; it is our consciousness manifest as Earth. Trust your body; let it speak to you. It is you, and because it is always present in the moment, it is a portal into the infinite love, wisdom, and energy available here and now. Let it show you what freedom is and where you can find it.

Use the affirmation "My body is safe" to reunite your mind, body, and emotions. Remember, it's safe to listen to your body, and you'll never lose your stories by letting them move. They might just move you.

I Am Presence

No matter what we are experiencing, there is one thing that we can always do, one choice that we can always make, and that is to be present. We can tune in to our own inner experience to notice the emotions, sensations, and thoughts that pass through us and are a part of us. Or, rather, that we are a part of. Presence is our point of access to the whole. It is where we must be in order to include more parts of the infinite within our experience.

Use the affirmation "I am presence" to return to an understanding that supports your creative cycles and the balance of your energies. The receptive state of rest, ease, and relaxation can be paired perfectly with the guided action of movement, of doing. Declare "I am presence" and invite yourself to expand. These words will begin a shift in your way of being.

Yes, you are present, but you are more than that; you are presence itself. What if instead of calling the thoughts, emotions, and sensations that we experience a part of us, we call ourselves a part of them? What is the source of our thoughts, emotions, and sensations? What is the source of the filter through which we perceive our lives? What is the source of the perspective that we call "I"? There is but one source of all things, one source that every part of us belongs to and that belongs to us: life.

Life is expressed in a myriad of forms, including matter, thought, and emotion, and as in any closed system, all parts of the whole affect the whole. The whole informs the parts, and the parts inform the whole. This communication flows both ways in a feedback loop of awareness. When we choose to be present, we are able to include more of our parts in our experience. I invite you to think of this process as deepening the experience rather than it growing larger. In presence, we are able to see the moving parts of our lives and how they fit together. We are able to see the relationships between our thoughts, emotions, and sensations, and it is in those relationships that we find clarity, answers, and direction. Presence is many things, including embodiment, returning to our intuition, healing, becoming mindful, and realizing our power to choose. Presence is our point of access to the infinite potential that rests within us: the whole.

There is no empty space, meaning that there is no separation between even the smallest of particles. Similarly, and following the same functional laws of energy, there is no empty space between thoughts, emotions, or sensations in the body. There is no space between the parts of our experience that we perceive as being separate. As soon as we deepen into the space, or the relationship between the parts, we are assuming the position of movement itself. The dance between the pieces of our experience is what we call *time*, and ultimately, it cannot be separated into moments. We are the movement of energy, we are the moment, we are time. Not only are we present, but we are presence itself. The affirmation "I am presence" will remind you not just of your ability to choose a perspective of being here, now. It will also remind you of the power in your true identity as time itself.

If you've ever been lucky enough to watch a forest, prairie, or any other ecosystem move through the seasons, you've witnessed the magic of a natural system organizing itself to harmony. There is nothing on the forest floor that is not beneficial to the entirety of the forest. Everything old becomes something new; everything dying is a gift for the living. If you've watched a forest turn, you've seen this with your own eyes. More so, you've probably realized at least once or twice, while standing among the giants, that you, too, are a part of this system.

As living beings, we are in a constant dance with all other aspects of our living planet and the living cosmos beyond. We can see, if we tune ourselves to perceive it, how we touch everything and everything touches us. Our connection with All That Is extends beyond just the physical, where the atoms of our body are literally in constant exchange with the world around us. We are connected with every single aspect of reality on every level of its expression. Our thoughts are a part of the larger mental plane. Our emotions are a wave in the sea from which all emotions are sourced. We watch as the systems in nature organize themselves to maintain balance, and we can watch this, too, within ourselves.

Presence allows us to deepen into the support of larger rhythms. As life plays each of us as a divine instrument, it never stops to check and see if we are in tune or on time. It just trusts us and adjusts us naturally, maintaining a constant pulse. We can learn to trust life too. When we choose presence, we begin to remember a deep truth: There is no separation between Earth's body and our bodies, Earth's mind and our mind, Earth's emotions and our emotions. We have the guidance of our Mother and life itself, and this is available to us at all times. Choose to access it. Use the affirmation "I am presence" to remind yourself that you are allowed to include as much of yourself as you choose in your awareness. Presence is the doorway to openness.

I Am Open

Every part of a system informs the whole, and the whole informs every part. As a part of humanity, Earth, the cosmos, and the patterns that extend even further, we are each a part of something larger than our individuality. Use the affirmation "I am open" as a reminder to choose to include information that comes from beyond the "self" within your experience. Some call it *channeling*, some call it *mediumship*, some simply call it *being human*. Each of these terms evoke something different for each of us as we hear them, perhaps bringing up curiosity or even resistance. I like to use a term that is more universally neutral; I like to call it *being open*. The practice of becoming open involves two key pieces.

The first is awareness. It is awareness that brings us closer to our goals and reminds us to stay on our path when we are tempted to stray. Becoming aware of who we are, and why we work the way we do as an individual, allows us to better work with our patterns and break out of cycles that keep us feeling repressed rather than free. Awareness of our own inner workings is also what gives us the insight we need to see how we fit into the bigger picture and thus how we can collaborate with those around us to bring our gifts to larger systems. When we connect with others who are expressing themselves authentically, our own truth is mirrored back to us. In order to stay centered in that truth, we must sustain our awareness. As we practice becoming and remaining aware of what is going on within us, or our inner experience, we also become aware of how we are connected to everything that is beyond us. Next, we become aware of how to include that information in our lives by opening up channels through which new information is able to travel.

The second key to becoming open is safety. It is through the practice of cultivating safety for ourselves that we are able to choose openness (a vulnerable state) without our physiological and psychological mechanisms fighting to protect us from danger. This is crucial. In an effort to stay alive by all means necessary, our systems will reorganize in any moment to ensure our survival. Awareness of our thoughts, feelings, and bodies frees us from the memories of the times when we were unsafe so that in the present moment we do not re-create the need for protection. Through this practice of creating safety, we come to find that fear itself is often what sends us into disruption.

The fear might come from an internal stimulus, such as a thought, or from an external stimulus, such as a sight, sound, or smell. Here, we can see the bridge between our internal senses and external senses and how our sensory experience is not limited to one or the other; bridges exist between the two. The bridge between our external world and our internal world is emotion. It is awareness of emotion, also known as *feeling*, that brings us into the position where we are able to access more of the information available to us in any given moment. The act of feeling allows us to be open.

Awareness is recognizing the emotional bridges between our internal experience and external experience. Cultivating safety for ourselves is important so that we can begin to make choices that break cycles and patterns of protection and move us gently into a state of freedom. So, how do we cultivate the safety necessary for openness to become our new normal? And why would we want to be open?

We create safety for ourselves in two ways. One is by noticing our triggers, be they external or internal, and introducing an alternative response. This is a practice, as all things are. Be easy with yourself. The first step to moving from a reaction or protective response into openness, or a heart-centered response, is to validate any emotion that comes up by allowing ourselves to feel it fully. As we do this, we will notice that the roots of the emotion come into our awareness. We might have memories come back to us that show us the cause of the trigger or the initial experience when that emotion was not allowed to be fully felt and integrated.

The intention of being open helps us create the space for ourselves to fully feel everything that comes up for us. It often asks us to slow down and include less in our experience so we are not rushing through our feelings to get to an ever evolving-destination. Feelings don't always need us to stop what we are doing, but they do require a certain level of focused attention, which can mean pausing and taking time to step away from a task or conversation to honor our need to be present with ourselves. Giving and doing are beautiful things, but if we are giving and doing in place of feeling, things get out of balance.

This lack of integration in the moment that an emotion arises is perceived as our inability to feel through the emotion to its completion. This is what causes a pattern to begin in which the emotion will come up again and again in response to a trigger. We free ourselves when we allow ourselves to feel, and we feel when we know we are safe enough to do so without being harmed. Choosing to feel is synonymous with both openness and self-love. As we create a safe space for emotions to be felt, we are validating them. We allow them to inform our system and then transform into something else. They do their job, and then they go off the clock.

This practice of feeling is what brings us out of patterns of thought and behavior that keep us continually choosing protection rather than freedom. Choosing freedom is where we will see movement in our lives that looks like synchronicity, support, opportunities, self-development, and healing. Remember, your story is yours to keep, and how you tell it is your choice. It is always safe to release an experience to your past so that you can be free in the present. I liken this to walking around with a filter. If we are holding on to parts of our past that we did not feel safe enough to feel (integrate) in the moment, then we introduce that old filter to all new experiences, and we make each new choice from that place of not feeling safe. When we release our past, we come into each new moment fresh and clean with our true, authentic desire and our own heart as our compass.

The second way we create safety for ourselves is by taking inspired action. When we notice something in our external environment that is not supportive of our true self, we are prompted to change our environment. This is internal work, but it is also external. This often involves restructuring the relationships that we have with people, substances, media, and other aspects of our lives. Noticing how we are functioning in relationship to everything we would consider to be separate from us can show us which things resonate with our deepest intention of being love and which do not.

Keep in mind that something may be resonating with you that is actually not beneficial to you. It is common to live in environments and make choices that resonate with any number of old wounds before those wounds are recognized, released, and integrated. Awareness and intention are the power combo for healing, because when they are paired, the wounds trust that the present moment is safe enough for them to alchemize into their gift. This process of alchemy opens channels that bring us new, refreshed energy.

Any number of large or small changes to our external environment can provide the safety we need in order to include more information from the vast whole that we are a part of. This is a process, and as our awareness of our inner world increases, it includes becoming aware of what action we can take to support ourselves.

Use the affirmation "I am open" to set the intention for yourself to be a channel for whatever love intends to bring to you and through you. Love is the most powerful creative force that exists; it creates space, it bridges seemingly impassible gaps, it joins and unites. Love brings balance. Love is the force of collaboration. It is the wisdom that brings solutions to problems with ease and minimal effort. It is support. Love heals.

To choose openness is to commit to yourself. When you're choosing to allow yourself to become the channel for everything you need, you are laying down your weapons, your shields, your armor—the patterns of thought and belief that hold you away from your fullest expression. You are becoming lighter, quicker, and more able to respond to shifts in your environment. You will find new understanding as to how you relate to what is around you and how you connect with your own past. Openness will free you so you are able to move into your most authentic self and find the means of expression that allow you to share your gifts with the world.

Choosing to be open may feel unsafe at first, but in time, this feeling will change. You will be open enough to receive the guidance in each moment that actually keeps you safe, here and now, rather than missing cues of potential danger or dis-ease in your current environment due to being stuck in the past. Openness brings clarity. Openness restores the trust that you have in yourself to navigate your life.

I Don't Know

"I don't know" is not at odds with "I know." In fact, one could not be true without the other. However, when we declare our unknowing, we are consciously opening ourselves up to receive all parts of ourselves that we have yet to understand in this life.

Imagine life through the perspective of a spider. A spider may live in the same room as you or me and hold a perspective so different from our own that we may not recognize their world and ours as even being shared. Now, imagine the perspective that your neighbor holds and know that their world may look equally foreign to you because you hold a different filter up to life. This filter is completely unique to you and is built through your own life experiences. What is it then that we have in common with both the spider and our neighbor? We all have the ability to receive, interpret, and express emotion.

Emotion is the fabric of the universe, often called *energy*. And we, as receptive and interpretive beings, feel it. Emotion may be routed through one creature's system completely differently than it moves through another's, and yet, both are living as feeling beings. Both belong to the web of emotional energy.

When we declare "I don't know," we honor the myriad of experiences that are not our own in this life and this body. We recognize, simultaneously, that there is value in separation and in wholeness and that both values equate to the same. When we state "I don't know," we are also stating what we do know. We state that there is value in time and the unfolding of our stories. We accept where we are in the moment, and in doing so, we open ourselves up to include more information within our awareness. We know that we can come to understand anything and everything that our curiosity leads us to. We release the pressure to have more information than we have now or to be somewhere we're not, and in doing so, we resonate with the love of self-acceptance. We affirm that our lives are guided by more than what we know, and in this understanding of guidance, we release the need to understand anything more.

The affirmation "I don't know" is a declaration of trust: Trust in our worthiness to receive understanding. Trust in the timing and direction of our lives. Trust in the bigger picture that we are all a part of. When we are in the thick of the dark and the throes of the drama, we can state to ourselves "I don't know" and feel the security that comes in trusting that we are fully equipped with the tools to navigate our lives regardless of whether or not we fully understand what's going on. The greatest of these tools is compassion.

In extending compassion to the spider, to our neighbor, and to ourselves, we are once again simply stating, "I don't know," and furthermore, "I don't have to." We don't have to understand anything to offer compassion, and it will always heal, direct us toward the highest good of all, re-center, validate, and clear emotional stagnation to put us in a balanced position of service to all. From here, we can take both direction and action that is guided by everything beyond our knowing.

I invite you to affirm "I don't know" and, in doing so, to open yourself up to all the parts of you that you've yet to meet or have forgotten. Let this affirmation bring you the relaxation that you need in order to trust and enjoy life and to offer compassion to yourself and all with whom you share this world.

I Know

Stating "I know" can be as useful as stating "I don't know." These words can remind you that the more expanded version of you does have the information that you wish you had in a moment of not knowing. You may not yet have the tools to access the information in the moment you desire it, or maybe you do. Either way, you can rest in the emotional peace that comes with understanding you have exactly what you need now to navigate from the present. You also, in choosing to relax, open yourself up to receive, which gives you the best chance possible of actually bringing more information through for yourself. Use the affirmation "I know" to remind yourself that you are both limitless and limited, and to accept your current limitations as the perfect place to work from.

There is an aspect of you that is as real as the one you call "me" but bigger. This version of you has access not just to that which is illuminated by your awareness, but also to the entirety of your darkness. It is important to note that darkness is not bad. It is simply that which you cannot see. When you merge with the version of you that knows you fully, you invite more of your darkness into the light. The "you" that you are familiar with grows to hold more information, more ideas, more energy, and more love to share with the world around you. Use the affirmation "I know" to invite the version of you that you call "me" to merge with the larger you that exists just beyond the current scope of your awareness. You are so much more than you know.

I like to call the more expanded version of myself *the dreamer*. I call the version of me who identifies with my name as well as the world she lives in *the dream*. It is imperative to me that I remember myself to be both. But, if I am the dreamer, why would I dream limitations for myself? Consider that you are water (you actually are), but in this case, imagine yourself as a river. You have an origin and a destination, yet you are a part of something much larger. Not only are you the same water that inhabits the clouds and the oceans, but you are also the molecules that break and rearrange to become the H_2O you know yourself to be. As you travel from point A to point B, you are reborn a million times. You exchange particles with the rocks you pass over, you evaporate, you are joined by the rains. You go through so much change. All the while, as you craft your own path to the sea, there is something that prevents you from leaking. For, if you were to leak out with no bounds, you'd become the soil around you. There'd be no travel, trajectory, or movement through the landscape of your life. Thankfully, the riverbanks hold you accountable to your goal and keep you within the bounds of a healthy flow. Thankfully, you have boundaries. Gratefully, you are limited.

Use the affirmation "I know" to remind yourself that beyond your limitations you are truly limitless. Beyond your humanness, you are more. Beyond your darkness, there is a version of you who holds the awareness of your entirety. Beyond your darkness, you are light. Beyond your not knowing, you know. We can thank the limitations of our lives and, in doing so, offer them the opportunity to support us even better. This affirmation asks us to take the opportunity to reorient ourselves to an empowered state of gratitude. From here, we know.

I Am the Prayer

Your prayer is your voice. In this way, every affirmation is a prayer, and every word is an affirmation. You speak life into yourself. You are the prayer.

The prayer is the start. To pray means to communicate with something larger than your own little self—a conversation with what lies beyond your personality or ego. We pray when we talk to the trees, when we let life direct the movement of our bodies, when we experience the rapture of pleasure, when we laugh, when we cry, when we create, when we let it out.

We pray when we communicate a dream—unfiltered, often messy, and raw—directly to the energy of life; we open up a channel through which it can be born. You can pray to anything or anyone that feels bigger than your little self. This can be any version of God, a higher version of yourself, the earth, Spirit, Life, Love, etc. All that matters is that you pray to someone or something that you believe has the power to hear you.

The reason prayer works is because it allows you to shift into a position where you're not gripping for control. In fact, this is why so many of us feel our prayers go unanswered. When we pray in a way where a certain outcome is needed, we shut out every other miracle that could come to us. We restrict the channel of creation by holding on to control. When we grip, the pieces of life are not able to move. We hold them in place, thinking we know what is best. True prayer says, "I trust you. I trust that love has the power to create the highest outcome. I trust that love has a vision more expanded than my own. I trust you to move me."

With this said, we can pray for or about anything. Our prayer can be wordless or a many-page entry in a diary. I prayed this way for years, pouring my heart out to my journals before I could even fully believe that there could be something larger than me directing my life. However much I wanted to trust in a force beyond my little self, I was afraid to give up that control, and I felt the effects of that in my life. Luckily, life brings us many opportunities to learn how to let go. Sometimes we fight to maintain our illusion of power, but as soon as it is stripped from us, we rejoice, remembering that there is so much more. Finally able to set down the burden of doing it all alone, we accept assistance and return to our true power.

If any of this sounds abstract to you or brings up resistance, just roll with it. Try the practices in this book and see how these new understandings anchor in your own life when given the opportunity. This is one of the things, like most things, that the mind cannot fully grasp but the body knows. Your body is an instrument of Earth and a tool for creation. Our bodies have the power to reorient us to truth as we learn to listen.

As you work with this book, you'll be coming back to a way of being where you are able to receive the subtle direction of life through your body. This is where the prayer starts to go both ways. You speak; you put your dreams into motion. You listen; you receive the guidance to create them. All that is required is practice and a dedication to cut out the extra noise in your life that limits your ability to hear yourself clearly.

Use the affirmation "I am the prayer" to remind yourself that you are already speaking to what is beyond you and your words have power. You can choose to pray with intention so that your ability to create expands. It's worth a try, and you are strong enough to handle everything that comes along the way.

I Express Myself

Each of us experiences a personal truth that belongs to us alone. It is subjective and unique. I invite you to use the affirmation "I express myself" to continually make choices in the ever-present moment that create the circumstances necessary to recognize and open channels for your self-expression.

We've talked about cultivating the safety necessary to create openness. We've talked about the importance of making space for our thoughts and feelings to be expressed within our own minds and bodies. Now, we can take this one step further to explore what it might look like to let those thoughts and feelings out in ways that create balance, beauty, and an example of authenticity that shows others that it is safe for them to express themselves as well.

We create barriers to self-expression when we don't feel safe. Perhaps we are afraid that if we are truly seen we won't be accepted or that there won't be a space for us. We might fear that our inner truth will break something if it doesn't fit into the prescribed mold. We might fear that we are too much or not enough or even that we are broken or missing pieces. We might believe that our truth will be taken from us if we express it. Love is here to change all of this. Let us remember that fear is not the enemy but rather a valuable part of ourselves that expresses through us in order to show us that we have, again and always, the opportunity to choose love.

When we choose to express beyond our barriers, we are consciously and actively choosing love. We are bringing our fears into the light of awareness so that they may tell their stories and transform into their love-based counterparts. Love is the power, the fuel behind the change that we wish to see in our lives and our world. All we have to do is choose it, and that power of choice can never be taken from us.

There will be moments that self-expression looks simply like allowing our thoughts and emotions to exist within our own bodies and minds. The expression is the feeling. It is here that we find anxiety unravels. Rather than feeling a pressure to organize and make sense of our inner experience, we simply choose acceptance. By accepting our thoughts and emotions, we are saying yes to ourselves. We are listening, and by listening, we are affirming, "You deserve the space to speak, and you deserve to be heard." This is an incredible act of self-love. This choice will begin to reorganize not only our internal patterns of thought and belief but also our external environment, as our choices are now completely infused with the light of our inner awareness.

It is truly each of our individual responsibilities to share our inner world. This is how we create! I invite you to use the affirmation "I express myself" to guide you as you take a look at the walls that you have built around your heart, then choose self-expression as the means to bring them down. Each brick in your wall is made of something valid and valuable, something that, when acknowledged, will transform into a great gift. Let it out! Together we can celebrate our differences and realize that no matter our personal context we are all working, whether we're aware of it or not, toward remembering our truth as love.

Oftentimes, our thoughts and feelings do not fit into our current model of understanding. That's okay. As we allow ourselves the freedom to think and feel whatever we think and feel, we find that our belief structures shift to make space for our truth to be heard and experienced in new ways. Due to the nature of creative energy, we will also find that our external environment begins to shift to create new opportunities for our expression to be received by the world around us.

So, we might start with just noticing our thoughts and feelings and saying to ourselves, "I don't understand this, but here it is." This alone changes our energetic pattern of movement, or frequency, to align with new opportunities for self-expression. You'll find that this practice of listening to yourself will magnetize others to you who are also willing to listen. It will bring you artistic means and the support that you need to explore them. It will gift you the curiosity and passion that feels like the fire of aliveness within you that directs you toward the types of self-expression that will set you free.

Through self-expression, we can choose to allow our lives to unfold in ways that uproot patterns of thought and create not only new behaviors but also new life circumstances and potential futures that fit our biggest, brightest dreams.

Ask yourself, "What dreams do I have in hibernation?" The question will begin to wake them up. Dreams feel like aliveness. They feel like something calling you forward into a new space. Naturally, this process of becoming free will bring up our fears and limitations. It will show us all of the thoughts and the patterns of thought that tell us that we cannot be our fullest, most vibrant selves. It will say things like, "There is no space for you"; "You are wrong" or "You are too much" or "You are not enough"; "You can't heal"; and "You are the only one." This is an important voice. This is your subjective truth, and it deserves the space to be felt and heard and expressed through your thoughts, emotions, art, movement, and voice. Express it however you can. Give it permission to move through you and move you.

I like to thank my fear when it arises. I thank it for holding my hand and showing me the way back to love again and again. I thank it for its patience with me. Fear is a filter through which we see the stories we tell ourselves, and it brings us the opportunity to choose to tell our story differently. Use the affirmation "I express myself" to choose to allow the stories within you to find their way out. Choose to let your walls fall down as the voice that speaks from within them creates a new way.

I Am Unique

Consider that consciousness doesn't just belong to each of us individually but rather is something we share. Everything we experience as physical and everything beyond that, the nonphysical, are all interconnected parts of this vast sea. Each of us occupies a point of awareness within consciousness. This point is uniquely our own. The place you see and experience the world from is yours and yours alone. We won't talk about shared consciousness here because it is a topic that deserves the time and space to explore it deeply. However, I will say that even when consciousness is shared (think telepathy), your point of awareness still belongs to you. The experience you create is not happening anywhere else. Use the affirmation "I am unique" to remind yourself of the great value you bring to life itself and the world around you simply by occupying a perspective that only you can.

No one can take your perspective away from you. And there is no reason to attempt to occupy someone else's point of awareness. In other words, you can't be anyone but you. And if you could, the world would be missing out on you. Life is full, robust, healthy, and beautiful because of the diversity that is brought by each of our unique perspectives.

Remembering this helps us reclaim our energy from the effort of trying to be like someone else or trying to make someone else more like us. This affirmation helps us remember the value of our uniqueness and theirs. Even if someone doesn't agree with you, even if their perspective causes harm, their perspective is of equal value to yours—and yours is of equal value to every other perspective. This is not the type of value that is attached to outcomes but rather the inherent value that comes from each of us being a part of life and allowing life to live, learn, and grow through us.

In recognizing our uniqueness, we remember that there is no competition. The efforts once placed on being right fade into the unity of being one great being with infinite faces. We prioritize our self-expression and see it as an invitation for others to see as we see rather than a force that says, "Be like me or you're wrong." We regain our access to the health that we all receive when each individual is thriving in their own unique way. We must simply be love so that all others are encouraged to meet their highest potential and contribute their unique gifts to the whole. This is beyond the personal judgment of good, bad, right, and wrong. It is our great power and responsibility to be love regardless of our judgment of the way others are doing things.

We can completely disagree with the way someone is living and still treat them with compassion, trusting that life itself will express through them as it needs to. We can set appropriate boundaries that keep us safe, possibly even keeping people away from us entirely, trusting that if this is a compassionate choice for the self, it is a compassionate choice for the other, regardless of if they agree with us or understand the decision. Choosing to be love is the highest and most nourishing choice. It always creates the best outcome, and we never need permission to choose it. If we wait for someone else's behavior to be what we deem as worthy of love, then we keep ourselves from being who we truly are (love) until the other person gives us a permission slip that belonged to us all along. When we withhold love, we limit our expression, and therefore, we limit our influence. When we withhold love, we are unable to be love. There will always be people whose perspectives are so far distanced from our own, so harmful or hateful, that we cannot even fathom how they could live in such a way. Even here, we have the opportunity to meet others with loving acceptance and choose compassion. Acceptance doesn't mean allowing something to stay the same. It means being honest about what is happening so that we can meet each moment with presence and therein receive the most inspired action. This is how we allow love to work through us. Quite contrary to things staying the same, love offers itself as the most powerful creator of change.

Each of us has a unique role. By being us and not trying to be anyone else, we prompt and generate love to behave in the ways needed for the whole of collective consciousness to be nourished and restored to ease. Allowing this bigger-picture perspective to enter our way of thinking can be immensely helpful in times when we are personally hurt by the way someone else sees us or behaves in the world.

There is no one else who can compromise your space and no need to compare your path to that of another unless it inspires you to be more of yourself. You can rest into your own rhythm, timing, and journey by remembering that it is literally impossible for anyone to take your uniqueness away from you. You've come as you are, on purpose, and no one else can take your spot.

Invite the affirmation "I am unique" to join your beliefs so that you can focus on what it means to be uniquely you as an expression of life, as an expression of love. Here is where you will do your best work, make your impact, and find fulfillment. Not a drop of your energy will be wasted when you dedicate your entire life to becoming more of who you came here to be. It is only in the commitment to being yourself that you position yourself as fully able to contribute your unique gifts to the world.

As with every affirmation in this book, these words can serve as a sign pointing you inward, asking you to check whether or not the stories you carry are aligned with your deepest intention—the intention that lives at your core, the intention to be your own unique, authentic expression of love. You can bring these words to life each time you feel the need to change someone else or change yourself to be more like someone else. It is your responsibility to check the expectations you hold for yourself and others and make sure they are truly yours. This is powerful, life-changing work, and no one else can do it for you.

There Is Space for Me

If you've ever felt like there is no space for you to be yourself or that you're missing your group of people who feel like your chosen family, you're not alone. Many of us go through this on our way to becoming seen and loved for who we truly are. Like all things, this is a process, and it requires something from you. Use the affirmation "There is space for me" to remember that you create space for both yourself and your creations by being who you truly are.

We live in the juxtaposition of wanting to both fit in and stand out. The desire for uniqueness is innately built into us due to the simple fact that we are one of a kind. There is not another person on this planet who occupies the same perspective as you do. Therefore, your expression is entirely unique just because it comes from you. It comes through you as a portal between the imagined and the tangible. You are the only one who can offer your perspective to the rest of us. And we need it. Otherwise, we're trying to do a puzzle without all of the pieces.

"There isn't enough space for me" is an out-of-tune belief that doesn't harmonize with our deepest truth as love. Love shows us that there is enough space for everything that we bring to the table. Love shows us that we can have our full experience in any given moment without rejecting any of it. What would it look like for you to show up fully in your life? Your full commitment to your authenticity will change what you believe is possible for yourself. When you choose to allow your fullest expression of self in each moment, you arrive at each locked door with the key of your authentic self. You haven't really tried if you haven't really tried as you.

The lesser characters we play can arrive in myriad forms and with unending methods to try to show us who we truly are. Despite their duplicitous appearance, even these inauthentic roles we play serve the intention of love. Love which desires above all else to remind us to be love. Love which reminds us that it is the essence of who we are. Love that approves of our authentic, unique expression of ourselves. Love which desires us.

The authentic self is the self that arrives in full confidence. This version of you doesn't ask to take up space; they simply do. Not in a grotesque way. You're not skipping the line or breaking any universal rules. You're not taking space away from anyone else. There is simply a space that belongs to you alone that no one else can fill. You either fill it or leave it empty. If you leave it empty, there is something missing. Unconsciously, others will try to fill it to bring fullness and restore the full sound of life's chorus. No matter their efforts, no one can replicate what is solely yours to contribute to this world. You either let us have it, or you don't. What a shame it would be if you tricked yourself into believing that there wasn't space for you. What a terrible loss.

You may be assured that the simple fact of your existence is proof that you are worthy of taking up space. Your desires are worthy, your heart is worthy, your mind is worthy, your body is worthy. There is no part of you that is not worthy. Because you exist. This affirmation asks a lot of you. It asks you to arrive courageously in each fresh moment, offering yourself the presence of self-love and radical acceptance. It asks you to say yes to the fullness of your experience, to stay here with the parts of you that feel like too much. It asks you to reorganize your life to create the space that you now know you deserve. It asks you to remind yourself that not only is your desire divine, it is needed.

Not only is your authentic expression needed, it is your responsibility to offer it to the rest of us. It asks you to deconstruct the walls, barriers, and boundaries that pose a threat to your success. It asks you to dismantle the stories that say you can't and to challenge the notion that upholds your lack, flaws, unmet expectations, and failures. "There is space for me" asks you to remember your perfection now—not out there when you hit the target, not when you achieve or overcome, but now. You are worthy of being yourself now. Your creations, which are your self-expression, create the space for you. Don't wait for the space to show up first. Create what is yours to create—that is, whatever you desire—and watch how the space appears.

I Am Safe to Feel

There was a time music tried to kill me. I was terrified of it. I hated it. Although I loved it deeply, I couldn't stand it. I hated that there was anything that could take hold of my emotions and carry me into a lost world, seemingly alone, with no support. How dare music do this to me, to anyone? Who did music think it was? I'd avoid the radio. I'd keep it off. I'd choose silence. Because at least this way, even though I was giving up the most meaningful thing in my life, I was in control. The truth was, I didn't want to go where music wanted to bring me. I was afraid that it would transform me and I wouldn't come back. Which was exactly true. What I didn't realize was that I wouldn't want to come back—back to the scared, insecure version of self that was dying. What I also didn't realize is that she would die either way. Her future was calling, and there was no avoiding it.

At that time, the music was a risk I couldn't take. I was in between one life and the next, not sure of who I was and entirely afraid that the emotional provocation of someone else's experience could sing me right into an identity that wasn't my own. I wasn't sure where to find myself, so the idea that I might fall into an emotion felt dangerous. I most certainly did not feel safe within myself. I was using numbness to attempt to keep myself safe from what was there. I knew music could make me feel, and that felt like a threat.

In this personal season of feeling lost, of being between one identity and the next, I began to ask myself questions that I later realized marked the beginning of my journey in rebuilding self-trust. I found myself asking why things happened and wanting to know what part I played. If I was to feel safe with myself, I would need to know that I could trust my own decision-making. I wanted to know that whatever blocked me from perceiving danger in the past could be cleared now in the light of my awareness. I learned that our emotions can't hurt us, intelligence is not in the mind but rather in the heart, and emotions move with incredible self-direction when allowed.

Have you ever asked yourself "Why did that happen?" This basic query is answered by filtering our experience through a series of thoughts that can collectively be called a *belief*. Our beliefs are the means through which we assign all meaning to our experiences. Our beliefs create our identity, or ego—the person whom we are referring to when we say "I" or "me."

When we begin to deepen our senses, we realize that this "I" is just a small part of the larger being that we are. In order for the identity, or the "I," to stay intact, it must continually reinforce itself. Think of it as a structure that is undergoing constant threat and must repair itself to stay standing. The main goal of a belief is to reinforce the identity, and it will do so until it is questioned.

The moment that we recognize a belief is the moment of questioning and a great moment of power. We are empowered because we can then make a choice, and the ability to choose in each moment is our ultimate power as creators.

How would your life change if the beliefs that kept your identity intact started to fall? What if we stopped affirming beliefs like "This is who I am and who I will always be," "I do not deserve it," "I am only able to experience this much and no more," or "I am guilty, bad, or broken"? What if we recognized the power we have to choose how we talk to ourselves?

When our beliefs rise from the shadows of our subconscious into our conscious awareness, we have the opportunity to change them by replacing them with new affirmations of health, well-being, worthiness, trust, and love, which are our true identity. The practice of changing our beliefs is as natural as reinforcing them, and all that it takes to do so is the bravery to recognize and question what we believe to be true about ourselves, others, and our world as a whole. When we enter into this practice with the willingness to let it all fall to love, love will guide and reorganize not only our own lives but our entire world.

When we do this work, we are really looking at relationships: the relationship between self and other, between inner experience and the outer world, and between the pieces of our world that create larger systems. This work creates a healthy relationship with self that simultaneously expands to create healthy relationships between self and everything that self interacts with.

One self-loving thought turns into an action and then invites a self-limiting belief, be it our own or that of another, to shift as well. Imagine that no matter where you are you treat everyone with absolute compassion, non-judgment, and love while still maintaining your own healthy boundaries. What would you need in order to behave that way in any environment? You might say "Mental health" or "To feel safe" or "To have a good sense of intuition or inner direction." All of these are necessary.

To behave in a way that is both knowing and loving, we must feel safe. We must cultivate a sense of safety that comes from inside of us and can be carried with us into any environment and situation that we encounter. From this sense of inner safety comes a strong intuition or inner direction, which tells us where our boundaries need to be. Similarly, we find mental health when we follow the same roots back to the core part of us that exists as pure potential.

How, then, can we cultivate this feeling of safety so that our lives can naturally reorganize to balance and create more balance in our world as a whole? We can allow our emotions to move freely within us. We can let our thoughts do what they will and know that we are not them, for we are the one who thinks, who watches, who observes, and who has the power to choose to give attention to our thoughts and strengthen them or to let them pass.

Our emotions will always tell us which thoughts and beliefs are life affirming and which are life draining. If it feels like love, joy, magic, expansion, and freedom, then it is worth keeping and nourishing. Thoughts that feel like this reflect our more expanded, true identity, and they will cultivate the sense of safety that allows us to live, feel, and express ourselves authentically. If a thought feels like fear, anxiety, tightness, or defensiveness, then it is worth lovingly questioning.

We don't have to move, sort out, or organize our thoughts and emotions, because they move on their own. As your emotions regain their freedom, they will show you their intelligence and self-direction, and they will effortlessly reorganize every system of your being to balance. This is where healing happens. This is how we heal our world. Through feeling, we find true meaning, true power, and true safety.

Remember, this is the process through which we find true strength in our vulnerability. We can supplement our feeling of safety as we restore its innate position in our lives. It can take time to reestablish safety as the foundation of our guidance system, and the support we build for ourselves in the interim can allow us to make choices that truly feel like our own. We get to build our network of support on purpose.

When I was afraid of music, I didn't feel safe enough to be vulnerable. The waves of emotion that music could invoke felt threatening. I worried they would grow too big, too strong, and carry me away. My journey was slow and long, and oftentimes I wanted it to be faster. I learned to do everything I talk about throughout this book as the method behind my own healing journey. I built, with my own two hands and my powerful imagination, the structure of support that I needed in order to bring myself back to a sense of safety.

I had to learn to believe that I was strong enough to feel. I had to remember. I had to choose to place myself in situations and around people that could remind me. It wasn't something that could happen all at once. But over time, with a dedication to my intention to experience the full life ahead of me in a way that felt free instead of scared, I began to move. I never needed to find the courage to take on the full journey; I just needed to take one little step at a time.

As time carried on, I not only regained the strength needed to listen to music, but I also deepened my commitment to using music to express myself and direct the emotional energy of both myself and others. I reclaimed it. I made choices to strengthen my musical skills, like studying guitar, piano, songwriting, and music theory. I'd always had a passion for sound and what it could do. Ever since childhood, I'd written songs, performed, and stayed up late at night reading about artists I admired in teen magazines. Then, as I grew older, I let my dream of becoming an impactful musician fall to the wayside. Fortunately, my dreams didn't let me stay asleep. They called me back to life through my fear, my pain, and my lack of aliveness. The discomfort woke me up, and I realized that I had a choice. I was being invited to become more of who I came to this Earth to be. I chose to take my challenge as an opportunity.

Use the affirmation "I am safe to feel" whenever you notice a thought or feeling arise in you. Remember, this is not a dead end or an obstacle; it's an invitation into more of yourself. You can always move your center from your mind back into your body to find a safe, anchored space when powerful thoughts and emotions come up. If your body doesn't feel like a space to anchor, that will come with practice. That will come with choosing to feel and proving to yourself that you can, indeed, handle the waves.

This Is My Medicine

Everything in life happens for our liberation. We can choose to argue this perspective, and we'd be proven right, or we can choose to assume it to be true, and we'd be proven right as well. We are vast and can hold multiple truths. We understand that in assuming a belief—most importantly, a belief about the self—all internal functions either align in support of the belief if it is loving or to correct the belief if it is not. Either way, love guides. If we choose to believe that life truly supports and guides us, we open ourselves to receive that guidance and it becomes true. Use the affirmation "This is my medicine" to reorient yourself to the most loving potential available to you in each moment by assuming that all is happening for you, never to you or against you.

Living with pain for any amount of time, but especially chronic pain, is one of the most challenging circumstances a human being can face. Whether this pain is physical, mental, or emotional, it brings us to our depths, asks much of us and, in time, returns us to the surface of our lives with needed insights, growth, and healing that can be shared. It is up to us to make meaning from our pain. Only we get to decide if the pain is a punishment, a lesson, or an opportunity. Through my own process, as well as through the countless sessions I have done with clients around the world, I have seen the progression from victim-of-pain to pain-as-medicine. The shift is an integral part of the healing journey as we make our way toward integration—the place where we are able to meet our painful life experiences and the subsequent painful symptoms with full acceptance. Acceptance is the first stage of making our pain into our medicine. The wound is the way in.

At first, it may be something we curse. How dare this thing make us feel this way? Whether or not we believe that we "deserve" to feel pain is a question worth reflecting upon. We might decide that the wound is a symptom of us being awful or a symptom of our mistakes and shortcomings. Alternatively, if we don't believe we deserve to feel pain, we might decide that the wound is itself a mistake, that the world is out to get us, or that God got the wrong guy! Both of these mentalities are victim mentalities. And as long as you exist in the mentality of being a victim to your pain or life circumstances, you keep yourself at arm's reach from the cure.

My third child was born into pain. Within the first five weeks of his life, he endured both a brain surgery and a heart surgery. I spent the second half of my pregnancy learning to let go and exist in the vast unknown, as my son's prognosis was uncertain. At thirty-eight-weeks' gestation, I brought him into the world via planned cesarean section with the help of a large team of doctors. We went into his birth knowing very little about the process and what our baby would go through, because there are so many nuances that come with each individual's experience of hydrocephalus and heart defects. I'd watch him there, lying in his tiny hospital bed. I was unable to pick him up because dozens of tubes and wires covered his little body. He was intubated, which left him unable to cry or make any sound. He couldn't express his pain. It was hard in these moments not to see him as a victim. It was hard not to see myself as a victim. But I knew from what I had already been through that life only ever gives us medicine.

I felt his pain as my own, cultivating a new depth of empathy and understanding for those who have no voice to speak their own pain into the world. I realized that even in the most vulnerable state, even at the threshold of life and death, my son did not experience himself as a victim of his circumstances. He simply made his way through, never asking if he did something to deserve it or if it was all a big mistake. Everyone could see the wisdom in his eyes. Thomas knew that this was his medicine. And I knew as his mother how to teach him that it was. Not because I came with this knowing (although we all do), but because I forgot it and found it again through the gift of my own struggles.

I was challenged deeply in my own life. I was offered the chance to change my story about the reason "bad" things happen to people. I was offered many opportunities to take off the judgment of "good" and "bad" altogether. I wrote a song about this shortly after Thomas was born, a freestyle recording that ended up on my album *BETWEEN*, and I called it "The Scales." I was reminding myself and others that it is not our job to judge our experiences. It is our job to experience them.

Those were hard days, and arguably harder days came to follow as Thomas grew through illnesses, seizures, and many more hospitalizations. I had a lot of questions during that time, and I wove them through tears into prayers, songs, dance, and sometimes even screams. The questions I couldn't answer were wounds in and of themselves, a way inward toward the strength we all needed. As the mother, I was tasked with supporting each of my children through this time, not just Thomas.

The importance of my inner talk and inner tone became more obvious than ever before. I used the online fundraiser that I created as a deeply personal, public journal through which I shared our day-to-day experience with hundreds of others who came to follow my son's journey. Through these entries, I was cultivating awareness around my self-talk. I recognized how my words felt as I was writing them and chose, on purpose, to tell our story in a way that both asked for help and felt empowering. I learned that community is as equally woven by our asking for help as it is by our giving help to others. I learned to receive.

Sharing our stories is a way to alchemize our pain into medicine not just for ourselves but for others. You can start now. Tell one close friend or a diary. Speak a poem aloud to the wind or a body of water. It doesn't matter whom you share your story with; the act of expression itself puts you in the position of creator, and it is very hard to exist as both a creator and a victim at the same time.

As I was writing, creating, and talking to myself about what I was going through, I realized I had an incredibly powerful choice in front of me. I had the power to choose forgiveness. I could forgive life for giving us this challenge, forgive myself for handling it all imperfectly, and forgive others for being imperfect too. That, or I could keep myself a victim by fighting against each of these truths. Forgiveness is not submission; it is how we take our power back.

No situation, person, or circumstance can have power over us when we choose forgiveness. Forgiveness is what shifts us from being in a state of attempting to control what is out of control to a state of allowing love to work for us and through us. When we accept what has happened or is happening in our lives, we are not saying it's okay with us. We are simply stating that it is true and therefore positioning ourselves as empowered creators. We are choosing a state from which we are able to work with the resources we have available to us in that moment. We are giving ourselves a place to start.

We all need help at times. It's a normal part of being a human. It's important to cultivate relationships and communities that can support us and truly see us in our power even when we are going through hard times. It is important to uphold this vision of ourselves. We create strength within our communities by offering others the chance to rise to the occasion of helping us. We can always choose to ask for help from an empowered state. As victims, we ask others to affirm our victimhood. As creators, we invite others to participate in our creative process by contributing their gifts. The same request for help, no matter what it is, can be filtered through either lens.

Shifting from the mentality of victim to creator doesn't mean that we silence ourselves. On the contrary, we allow all of the voices that live within us to speak their truth. When they do, they make space for a higher truth that brings everything back into coherence. I filled many journals with "why me?" all the while knowing that I was writing with the intention of integrating my pain rather than amplifying it. Sometimes, being a creator looks like making something out of the voice of our inner victim. This has been the fuel for some of my best songs! Every part of you deserves to speak; just make sure that there is someone speaking back offering the love and reassurance that the hurt part of you needs to hear. Both voices can be yours. Both have value; both can exist without harming you.

No matter what our pain asks of us, being intentionally loving in the way we talk to ourselves about it is a key aspect of healing. Use the affirmation “This is my medicine” to begin to shift your story. Use these words to invite everything that has felt stuck to start moving. When you use the affirmation “This is my medicine,” you return yourself to a state of gratitude, trust, and relaxation. You choose to hand over your rigid illusion of control to your true power: the higher wisdom and rhythm of the life that lives you. In choosing this, even if you don’t know the “how,” you naturally tune yourself back into harmony with love, and the path unfolds before you, one step at a time. You have everything within you that you will need. Create a life that points you toward your inner resources and reminds you that you are whole.

My Imagination Is Powerful

Your imagination is not an unreal space. It is as real as what you can touch and hold, but it exists on a plane just parallel to and intimately connected with the one you can use your senses to experience.

The imaginal space is the birthplace of things. This is where our ideas take their first breath, where we do test runs and decide, whether consciously or unconsciously, to give more attention to something. This is where we decide which of our creations to feed and which to starve. Our imagination is where our dreams for our lives live.

Sometimes our dreams don't make it very far in the imagination because each time we begin to play with an idea, doubt comes up to suffocate it. Sometimes dreams live in the imagination for a long time, even for a lifetime, without ever being given a true chance to become reality, because we never learn to harness our power of imagination. However, the process is easy to learn, and with practice, you'll be amazed at what you can create. We're already using this process constantly, even if we don't realize it. When we begin to understand the power of our thoughts and emotions and how they work together, we remember the power of our imagination.

It's all too common to have a dream and, right along with it, a million reasons—or even one "really good" reason—to never make it our lived reality. But what if those reasons are based on something other than the truth? What if we can bypass this doubt with the process of imagination itself? What happens if we imagine ourselves to be the version of self that doesn't hold any of the beliefs that create the doubt that keeps the dream asleep? What if a version of us exists that can experience the dream becoming reality and all we have to do is become that person?

Imagination works similarly but differently for each of us. Some of us actually see with our inner eye, or mind's eye, when we imagine. Some of us hear, some feel, some simply sense, and some do it all. Typically, as we begin to strengthen our ability to consciously make what is imagined into our lived reality, we start with one or some of these skills being dominant and some being underdeveloped. Through practice, we can learn how to bring these skills online, and as we do, we become more powerful in our ability to manifest our lives intentionally.

We use our imagination to create the version of ourselves that can hold our dreams. We become the person we imagine whether we take ownership of this process or not. Imagining the person we want to be and speaking to ourselves as if we are that person opens up a channel of possibility that allows all of the pieces to come together for our dreams to become our reality. When we focus on what it would look like and feel like to be the version of ourselves that is living out our dreams, we attune ourselves to that version of self and flow right into being them. Feel the emotional state that you would feel if your dream was reality. Feel the joy, the love, the empowerment. Feel how the person who could hold this dream would feel. Become them.

Soon, you will find yourself accepting opportunities, finding help, and receiving insights that seemingly come from beyond you. This work reminds us that we are life itself; therefore, nothing is beyond orchestration. Life can put the pieces together for us when we open the mind and link the heart. Use the affirmation "My imagination is powerful" to remind yourself to dream big. The imaginal space is no space for limitations. Allow yourself to dream your reality into being. You're already using your imagination to create life; start to do it on purpose.

My Dreams Desire Me

Use the affirmation "My dreams desire me" to remember that your dreams for your life are coming through you because they desire to be lived. You are the vessel, the portal, the way that your divine imaginings are created in the world. There is no barrier to your creation of your dreams, no obstacles, just opportunities for fine-tuning, clarification, and building the inner and outer resources that you need in order to take the next step in your creation process.

When desiring the manifestation of a dream, we often look as far out as we can in an effort to assemble the pieces, test the water, and find the limitations so that we can work within them. By declaring "My dreams desire me," we can reverse this process. Let the dream call you into it. Instead of making each choice based on the limitations you project into the future, you'll reveal your path by your own movement, just as the banks of the river are carved by the water as it journeys toward the sea.

Your dreams belong to you and long to join with you in actualization, just as you long for their fulfillment. And because your dreams already belong to you, there is nothing you need to do to make yourself worthy of them. They are already manifested in a version of the future that you can choose. Instead of trying to come up with the energy and the path toward your dreams, just listen to them and they will both mobilize and guide you. The energy flow will reverse to work toward you, nourishing and energizing you as your dreams reach back and pull you forward.

Learn to listen closely and you will hear the dream whisper, "Quieter. Now, quieter still," as it invites you into the inner stillness required for its birth. This is the quiet space where the most subtle callings of your heart can reach you. As the mind gets quieter, the heart gets louder.

Recognize the feeling, the pulse, the sensation of love in your life, and you will know what is of the heart. The origin of the dream is enough for you to trust it. It is yours, it is not selfish, and you do deserve to experience it. Love shows us all of this. If a dream energizes you, it's leading you into it. If it feels like you have to come up with the energy by yourself rather than it springing forth from deep within you, it may be worth bringing it to question. Is this really my dream? Or is it coming from an unmet need? Either way, it will lead you into more of yourself. Neither is bad, but checking to see how you feel can initiate change that aligns you with desires on deeper levels, which places you on a path with even more meaning—the path of your dreams.

The heart is the only part of us that is equipped to process our pain. As much as the mind longs to understand the painful experiences we've been through, it makes a feeble effort. It crafts and re-crafts endless stories to create meaning from something that was destined to be a doorway and not a key. Pain is an invitation back into right relationship with all parts of the self. Oftentimes, our dreams are born from pain, but if we look deeper, we see here, too, that a dream inspired by its opposite is a dream born from a heart steeped in love.

Our dreams live in the dark, and we offer them light. Imagine you have a dream that is so far off in the future that you haven't even recognized it yet. It lives completely shrouded in the cloak of darkness, the part of you that you are unaware of. Then comes the light of your awareness, stepping closer. A part of the dream illuminates and comes into focus as you approach. You build it into your vision of your future and continue toward it. As you get closer, more and more of the dream shines with the light of your attention. Each facet guides you toward it as a beacon of your heart.

The path reveals itself, and all that it requires of you is to tune yourself back to love, again and again, as often as you notice that you have the opportunity to choose it. In time, you'll become so used to living in this loving state of being that any other state will feel jarring and disruptive. You'll know your power to choose love as well as the benefits of choosing it, and so, effortlessly, you will choose it. You'll keep yourself attuned to love and in doing so will naturally be called upon the path of your dreams, step by step. You don't need to focus on the darkness or squint your eyes to see more clearly. When you focus on what is illuminated, you will amplify this light, bringing more of yourself into your awareness. Love is light, and light is love. When your capacity to be love in human form increases, so too does your awareness. You will illuminate more of yourself because you are able to love more of yourself.

Use the affirmation "My dreams desire me" to connect with the part of yourself that exists in the future and has already experienced your dream being fulfilled. This version of you has no question about whether or not you're worthy of experiencing your dreams. They don't question how it will happen or when; they fully trust the process, given that they sit comfortably where all has been delivered and all is well. Perhaps it won't come together exactly as you imagine, but by connecting with this future self, two things will be true. One, you will experience the feeling of fulfillment in the present moment as you use your power of imagination to connect with the future. Two, you will then create from this frequency state, which naturally creates more of that feeling in your internal and external worlds. You will create a channel through which your dream can quite literally pull you into it.

To each of our dreams, we must show up in this way. We must show up for what is alive in us, what we are in love with, what bursts through us with every heartbeat, what dances with the pulse of our own life force, what life itself has fully endorsed. These dreams are worthy of existence because they belong to you, and you are worthy of existence. These are the dreams that we are talking about.

We set our dreams free by saying yes to them, even if they don't make sense and even if they present us with a challenging identity crisis. When we say yes to our dreams, the dream is then able to send the flow of inspiration back toward us. Each dream, no matter how small, asks to be honored and released to the love of acceptance. Therein, it can either transform to the most loving version of itself or fade away to make space for something more resonant with our deepest truth. Either way, our dreams give us valuable information by bringing more of who we are into the light of our awareness. Our dreams guide us into the dark.

It's normal to be afraid when we can't see. And as long as we are willing to follow the dream's guidance, we can safely take one step at a time toward a fuller and more fulfilled life. Our fear is not meant to stop us, and it doesn't have to. We can use our fear as an invitation to build our resources, support network, and skills. Whatever you do, don't let your fear become bigger than your dream. If it already is, then use the power of your imagination to start to minimize it, again connecting with the version of you that is already experiencing safety and success. If you're not sure what your dreams even are, then you can start here, with your imagination. Begin to visualize yourself happy. Piece together what that would look like, or even just what it would feel like, and then what it would require. You'll begin to do this work naturally as you quiet your mind and return to your heart.

Life has access to every part of us that is in the light and every part that is still in the dark. It brings us relationships, situations, and opportunities that are beyond what we can see and what we could have planned so that we can build out our path to our dreams. As long as we show up fully to each of these doors, they open, and with bravery and the willingness to face the unknown, we trust enough to walk through. When we give ourselves fully to our dreams, we give our full trust to life. We allow life to use us as life does—that is, without limitation. By recognizing that we are being magnetized by the divinity that exists both within us and our dreams, we allow the larger part of us to do this work with more ease.

Of course, heartfelt desire, despite its promise of success, does not ever claim to meet our personal expectations. These dreams come from a place so much more expanded than what we can imagine, it would be of our limited mind to think that we are able to direct their coming to fruition. We are in receiving mode when we are creating, although it appears we are the ones driving, taking action, and doing whatever is necessary to bring a desire to life. With a wider lens, we are reminded that it is life that brings our dreams to itself through us. Our best work happens when we can release the control that our ego grasps for and remember that anything and everything that feels like love as it moves through us will create such a different version of us by the end of its story that we cannot possibly imagine how it will turn out. It's okay to not know. It is safe to trust the process.

Use the affirmation "My dreams desire me" to relax into the joy of creating. In this mode of receiving life, we are moved by it in every way. This is your heartbeat, your power. This is you at your healthiest, happiest, most well state of being. It is here that you find your life's purpose and fulfillment. Purpose was never meant to arrive with the completion of a project or the meeting of a goal. You give your life purpose when you choose to create from the heart. Your purpose is happening now.

I Am Secure

Security lies in the open spaces, in the time that we give ourselves to truly be, to truly feel with no expectations. I invite you to use the affirmation "I am secure" to remind yourself that security is here in the present moment.

In each moment, we have access to the deep well of resources that springs forth from within us. The love that is present there is all that we need to guide us. We have talked about how to recognize love and allow it to inspire action. With that foundational understanding in place, we may now speak directly to the power inherent within us to support our dreams and desires.

Often, we meet our desires with a no before we even notice that they have arisen within us. In this way, our desires remain unconscious; we are unaware of them. When we find the space between the desire and the response to it, we find a wellspring of information that can direct and guide our experience. This is all we need to create the environment in which our desire can be born into reality.

Keep in mind that desires are like water. They shift and change their form as well as the boundaries and banks of the spaces that they flow through. They carry pieces of us along with them and deposit them where they are needed. Sometimes those pieces create blockages and make a home for unwanted inhabitants who stay until the debris is cleared. To keep the resources in our life flowing to where they are most needed, we must first see what is going on within us. We must know what it is that we are carrying.

Take the time to check in with yourself honestly and make space for all of your desires to declare their existence. We don't need to know why they exist or where they came from or even where they are going. When we allow them into our awareness, we are accepting our own wholeness—our unkempt, untamed wildness. We are allowing the fullness of who we are, of our experience, to exist. We are, quite simply, setting the stage for the manifestation of the highest desires each of us holds. We are allowing them to shift, move, reorganize, and integrate.

This process of self-acceptance is an honest one, and it requires a great deal of courage. But the reward is great. Because it is only through the process of honest inventory that we allow our desires to not only transform into their highest expression but also to transform us along the way. Through this process, we raise our frequency into love, and our desires follow suit. The old, egoic desires fall away in honor of the highest desires of the heart.

Can you hold yourself in a space that feels safe enough to be vulnerable? What do you need in order to do this? Is there something you can do right now, in this moment, to create that for yourself? Perhaps this looks like taking a moment of silence, speaking to the nonphysical, reaching out to a friend, putting yourself in a community space, removing yourself from a space that feels too tight for you, or shifting the way you tell your story. Whatever this is, be open to and present with the discomfort that may come with trying something new. Discomfort does not indicate a misstep; you'll notice this with practice and become familiar with your discomfort as you move through the process of restoring your inner guidance. No matter what comes up, feel it and remind yourself of the immense bravery it takes to do the work you are choosing to do.

Security comes from being safe within ourselves, not from external circumstances. We create the external environment of safety based on having security within. Security is about trusting our deep knowing, believing that our feelings are safe, and encouraging ourselves to make our best effort to be the love that we are in every given moment.

Perhaps the values you grew up with did not cultivate the willingness to be vulnerable that we need in order to experience true security. Luckily, we have the power within the present moment to choose a new way. We are revolutionaries. Each moment of honesty with ourselves is a protest. Each action we take to create a safe space for ourselves is an act of rebellion. We must do this work within as we are simultaneously involved in the systems outside of ourselves that we wish to restructure.

Acknowledge your desire to live in a world where you are nourished as much as you are feeding your community. A world where you are valued for existing. Where you are cared for and trusted and forgiven and where the resources that you need to support yourself and understand yourself are always available to you. A world where you are seen and heard. Imagine a world in which your place cannot be taken by another, where you are solid, steady, and rooted in your being. This is the world we say yes to creating when we make space within ourselves to listen to our desires with acceptance. Allow your desires to explain themselves to you, in as much detail as they offer, without demanding anything. When we stop pushing parts of ourselves away, we teach ourselves what security feels like.

Remember, ceilings are where we put them, and they are all made of glass, whether installed by one individual or a collective. They break easily as soon as we throw a stone or stand tall or heat the glass enough to melt them. There is no reason to keep a ceiling in place unless it is supporting you, and floors tend to do that job much better. So, find your roots, dig deep, and make space for your past to speak into the present so that your past may release you. See it as the ground that holds you up, the fertile soil made of ash from the burning old. If we create based on what has been possible in our past, if we continue to tell ourselves that we are who we were, we don't leave space to show ourselves a new way.

Be brave. Know that security travels with you and that you can find it in your breath, in the spaces between thoughts, in your sensations, and in your body. Open up to the fullness of yourself by allowing all parts of you to have a voice, and state, "I am moving, I am change, I am supported." And most importantly, "I am secure."

I Am Both

Just a month shy of twenty years old, I left a six-year romantic relationship that wrote the story of my adolescence and had become as much the core of who I was as I was. My newfound freedom dropped me off, bags packed and ready to explore, at the loading gate of the open world. Every part of myself that I had compromised for what I believed at the time to be "love" was coming back to me. This was real. Finally, I felt what it meant to be free. And simultaneously, my grief was so deep that I was drowning in my own shedding skin. I was forced to grapple with my expansion, and a part of me wanted to fight it. It would have been much easier if everything still fit in the boxes, if I hadn't outgrown my own skeleton, if I could just stay the same. Yet here I was, learning to hold multiple truths at the same time. I felt myself tearing, like the stretch marks of a belly bursting with new life. I was between, and I was both.

I invite you to use the affirmation "I am both" to remind yourself that you can hold many truths, emotions, and thoughts all at once, even if they do not agree with each other. You don't have to pick, but you can get curious. Let them stand to the question of love and see if they fall. Perhaps one folds into another, bringing it more life and beauty. Perhaps your larger truth as love knows how to direct all of the pieces of your experience.

It's safe to feel whatever you feel, to think whatever arises within your mind, and to let it all go. Because you are not these things. You exist beyond. Therefore, you may be assured that the full spectrum of your experience is safe. You can be both, and. There is always more for you to include within your blossoming identity and always more to release. When you approach your experience with love, acceptance, and curiosity, you make the space for yourself to both hold it all and hold nothing.

"I am both" reminds us that there is no need for thoughts to fight for space. If a thought feels crowded, it will come to our awareness for questioning, asking, "Should I stay?" It's not your job to put things in their places; it's your job to accept what is there and let it move. You are vast. You are the full spectrum and more. You contain many contradictions and opposites, and that is perfectly human. Center yourself in your heart and watch as your capacity to hold what is true for you expands.

I Am Responsible

It's easy to say we'd prefer a life where we are empowered, things happen for us, and we are the ones in control. Yet, many of us live our lives as victims of circumstance. In this way of living, the world has power over us, things happen to us, and other people are the ones in control. Given that we have the choice between the two perspectives, why would we choose to give up our power by choosing the latter? Use the affirmation "I am responsible" to remember that you are trustworthy and able to make great decisions. You can handle your inherent power to choose where you direct your attention. You are ready to reclaim the power that has been yours all along.

When we remember that we have the power to choose, there is one particular belief that will rise to our awareness. It is the one that says, "I am not responsible enough to handle this power," and usually, we agree with this, and so we find ways to give the power away. We say, "The people in power …," "The ones who control the systems …," "The ones who make me go to work …," etc., all the while neglecting the true power that we have to resonate with love and choose where we direct our attention.

The power to choose is one so great that many people simply choose not to acknowledge that they have it. The irony is that even this is a choice. We cannot escape our power, even if we try to give the responsibility to someone else. We are the ones who are choosing, whether consciously or unconsciously, to make meaning of our experience. So, why not take responsibility and begin to choose on purpose?

In order to do this, we must remember that we are capable and worthy of holding great responsibility. This means rewriting stories that are attached to old experiences of responsibility. Maybe we grew up having to be the responsible one and care for our parents or siblings. Or maybe our challenges with staying organized gave us the idea that we were irresponsible. No matter what the old stories are, we can bet that they will rise to the surface to be questioned as this belief changes. Let this process happen and meet yourself with love every step of the way.

When we remember our responsibility, we have to do some hard things. We often have to apologize. We have to remediate and repair. We have to cultivate the emotional and relational skills to be present with the experiences of other people. We have to admit to the hurt that we cause. But we also get to access something incredible that ultimately frees us: We reclaim our power to forgive ourselves. Additionally, we get to celebrate our successes fully in a way that we never could if we believed that things just randomly happen to us and have nothing to do with us choosing our own thoughts and emotional state. When we remember that we are responsible, we regain full access to our power to choose.

Use the affirmation "I am responsible" to remind yourself that there is an immense power in your choice, and you have this power, whether you want to or not. You are responsible, so claim it with certainty. Begin to access your power on purpose and watch how your life transforms.

I Forgive Myself

Self-forgiveness is the complete liberation of your energy. If you have ever seen a bouncy, joyful child and thought, "Wow, I wish I had that much energy!" you can be assured that you do! It's still within you. It is through a lifetime of repressing your truth, fitting into boxes, and becoming someone else's idea of a more loveable version of yourself that you have created dams to stop the flow of your own creative energy. Rather than your energy going outward toward life, it has gone inward in an effort to keep parts of yourself hidden away. It takes an immense amount of energy to punish yourself. Punishment is not a function of nature but rather something humans created in an effort to navigate expectations and control behaviors. It is entirely optional, and you can uncouple accountability from punishment within your own consciousness right now.

You are energy, pure and whole. There is nothing about you that can ever cut you off from the source of life that lives you. "I forgive myself" is an affirmation that reminds you on a cellular level that you are perfect, complete, and worthy. There is no part of you that you need to say no to, and in fact, when you begin to say yes, you get your energy back.

Remember, you have the power to choose which thoughts you give energy to. When you understand this, thoughts are no longer intimidating because they cannot control you. Your thoughts no longer get to do the job of directing your energy. Your mind becomes, again, as free as a young child but now with the power to amplify those thoughts that align with your deepest intention. You will now choose to think thoughts that uplift you, support your self-image, and remind you of your truth as an empowered, creative being.

When you say, "I forgive myself," you restore the trust in yourself that you lost along the way. We have all made decisions that we wouldn't make again knowing what we now know. However, the version of you that chose didn't choose with the understanding that you now have. You are currently remembering that you are a limitlessly powerful creator, and this drastically changes the choices you make. The past version of you is not who you are today, and through forgiving yourself, you release them. It is wise to let your former self die to the version of you that exists in this present moment. It is safe to do so, as nothing is lost. The past version of you deserves to be free to the past, not caged and carried along with you into each new moment. When you let go of your past self through accepting where you were then, you liberate your energy to come back to you in the present. You can set yourself free.

You are worthy of trust; you have an intuitive compass that guides your actions toward the highest good of all beings. You move with the pulse of the generative, creative whole. You are a gift to this world, and every perceived mistake you made is waiting for its new story. Tell it now. Reframe the past events that hold you hostage to yourself. Let your past self know that the current version of you is grateful for what you have learned. Find a space within you where you can truly rest in the gratitude of being alive, of being able to feel and experience yourself. You are gifted with the ability to learn and grow. Use the affirmation "I forgive myself" to step fully into your power now, the power of self-love and the transformation gifted by gratitude. Give thanks for the entirety of your human experience.

If there is guilt, let it be a doorway into your wounds. Be brave enough to step through, remembering that you are not what you feel but rather the one who feels. Create a container of safety for yourself so that whatever comes up has an out, whether this is through journaling, speaking aloud, painting, singing, dancing, exercise, or any other form of prayer. Guilt cannot keep your energy from you, and your intention to experience yourself fully includes both the guilt and the energy that it takes to keep yourself feeling guilty. Imagine how much energy is restored when you fully feel the emotion of guilt and let it transform into a higher harmonic of itself. You may choose to let your past hurt become your present gift. Through this alchemical process, you become the gift.

Forgiveness does not mean escaping responsibility. On the contrary, through forgiveness, we liberate our energy so that it is available for inspired action. Sometimes, repairs need to be made in order to restore harmony in the present. Our past actions may carry guilt because they created real harm. Separating punitive action from inspired action is a crucial step in restoring right relationship with the world around us. Rather than punishing ourselves, forgiveness offers an opportunity to be guided by a higher creative force: love. Love allows us to build and repair on a level that retribution can't even touch.

Use the affirmation "I forgive myself" to restore trust in yourself. Your inner guidance is always speaking, and this affirmation assists you in restoring your ability to tune in to it and listen. You are guided by the love that you are, and in each moment, you have the choice to let your past be your past. You have everything you need to direct your present action from a space of inner trust.

I Am Being Lived

The energy of life itself is living you. When you tap into this, you don't have to come up with your energy on your own anymore; instead, you receive energy flowing to and through you. This changes the way your life functions by restoring ease. All areas that were previously subject to restriction are freed and able to move with the innate wisdom of life itself. Use the affirmation "I am being lived" to remember that not only are you alive and not only are you life itself, but that life itself is what moves you.

We have a choice between two ways of living. Both are valid, and both will be made true by our choosing them. The first is to assume that life is a series of challenges meant to test us and make us stronger. From this perspective, joy is seen as a reward for accomplishing a hard-won victory through one's dedication to the pain and suffering required to stay alive. But what if we could choose to be dedicated to something else? The second way to live offers the opportunity to do just that. What if instead of agreeing that life is a burden to be overcome, we view life as the mobilizing force of creation and ourselves as what is being created? From this viewpoint, we are no longer the main character in a story oversaturated with other main characters. We become a beautiful and equally worthy aspect of a great being, something imbued with the ease, love, and health that we all long for. From this perspective, all that was out of reach becomes accessible. All that was something to be earned becomes our birthright.

So, try it on. Choose to include this affirmation in your life and see how it changes the way things work for you. Perhaps it is worth the challenge. Everything that must fall or restructure around you and within you to accept this new truth might just be worth the work. Because this is the work of life. And as soon as you say yes to this work, it finds the energy to do itself. No longer will you struggle and suffer, sputtering and trying, putting in effort, and finding patterns of self-pity and hatred when you miss your mark. No longer is the mark something out there, outside of yourself. When you choose to remember that life is living you, you become the reward. Again, you become the gift.

Use the affirmation "I am being lived" to declare your dedication to the energy that moves you. There is a way to become one with all that is and keep your individuality. Allow life to give you the gift of being alive and trust that the exchange is equal. Life is grateful that it gets to live through you.

I Am Right on Time

I invite you to use the affirmation "I am right on time" to trust the timing of your own process. I invite you to expand beyond any definition of slow, fast, or otherwise and to be assured that your timing is absolutely perfect.

Because it's not really about the timing. It's about being in tune with who you are. You can work for years toward something and never create the internal state that you need to actually receive it or enjoy it. Alternatively, you can illuminate a desire, walk toward it, and open a door that serves as a portal to your destination. It all depends on whether or not you are in resonance with love.

Of course, we oscillate as we find balance. You'd hardly be human if you didn't get caught up in the waves of your emotions or identify with your thoughts some of the time. When we embody a thought or emotion, we narrow the spectrum of our focus, like a laser beam. There is a distinction between embodying and identifying with an emotion or thought. Embodying is an important skill, but used without awareness, our experience of the thought or emotion can become our identity, and this limits the choices we make. Through the practice of remembering what love feels like for you, you will begin to identify with love itself rather than transitory thoughts and feelings. You'll respond to each new moment with the confidence of a person who knows they're right on time, and that alone will make this affirmation true for you.

We've all heard the stories that say we're late: We're too old to be this. There's not enough time left to learn that. Our peers have already accomplished X, Y, and Z, so why even try? We'd just be behind.

But what if we change the story? What if instead of believing that there is some external measure of comparison, we give up any effort to compare and release ourselves to the deep wisdom of our own process?

The first thing that will change is the seriousness. No longer will we walk through the day wearing time like a vice grip around our wrists and throats. Instead, we find the space to wear our hearts on our sleeves in place of a watch. All of a sudden, we will find a necessary ease, a powerful flow of energy akin to inspiration that will replace the clock as the mobilizing force in our lives. Where we once found doubt, lack, and reasons to stay small and hidden, we now find possibility. And this is enough to invite life back into everything we think and everything we do. We invite life itself to live through us, trusting that its timing, given its infinite potential and access to the whole web of existence, is much better than any timeline we could have personally come up with. This is especially true if the timeline we designed was mostly built on expectations that were never really ours to begin with. Now, we are willing to set down everything we picked up along the way. We are willing to set the clock down.

This new way of living asks us to confront the expectations of others. It asks us to examine what we hold true about our capabilities, what aging means, and where we have placed our glass ceilings. It asks us why we would want to hold ourselves back. Use the affirmation "I am right on time" to remind yourself that being trapped by time is a choice. You may break free from this illusion now and begin to create a life based on your own inherent timing. It's never too late to start; in fact, it's the perfect time. You don't have to be in a hurry, especially someone else's hurry.

This Is My Garden

There is something about tending to a garden that feels good at every stage. Whether it's planting the seeds, pulling the weeds, or harvesting the fruits, there is work or leisure to be enjoyed.

I invite you to use the affirmation "This is my garden" to appreciate the process of your life in every stage. Just as in the practice of gardening, we find seasons and cycles in our own lives. Some cycles move the waters of our bodies; some move our creativity, allowing it to flow out or rest within and gather new information. Some cycles help us heal by giving us time to build strength and self-love before bringing us a memory that points to the places in us that need release and new understanding. It is only through cycles that our innate wisdom can be applied to our lives and that our gifts can inspire the world around us.

When we tend to a garden, we have choices. We can focus on the leaves as they begin to spread further from the stalk and notice the space they move into. We can touch the buds, so potent in their color, tightly wound and waiting. We can observe the visitors who come to pollinate, and we can love the plants we nourish. We can focus on the beauty, or we can focus on the weeds. Our choice is in our focus.

While training to become an herbalist, my teacher, Jessica Belden, told me something I will never forget. She said, "All the medicine we need is growing right on our block, right here in the middle of the city. If only everyone could stop calling our medicine 'weeds.'" This brought me to think about how and why we label some plants as weeds. Is it possible that a plant is a weed until we understand its medicine? Or maybe the truest definition of a weed is simply something that impedes the growth of the plants we'd like to nurture. So then, how can we know with certainty which plants are weeds and which plants are worth keeping? How can we be sure in our own minds which beliefs deserve cultivation and which should be released? We must bring in the tools we've cultivated that allow us to both accept our beliefs and bring them to question. In doing so, we bring clarity to the spaces in our lives that aren't growing as we'd like them to or are so overgrown that we can't be sure what to pull and what to keep.

Bring the affirmation "This is my garden" into moments of uncertainty and doubt to shift your focus, own your power (which lies in your ability to choose), and choose gratitude for the opportunity to continue to grow. Focus on the flowers, and the weeds will wither. There are times in our lives when the sadness and strife are so intense that it feels as if our garden sees nothing but rain. In these times it can be helpful to look lower than the leaves and buds, lower even than the weeds. We can sink like water into the very roots of our being and ask questions there. We can ask what it is that our soil is made of. What is it that nourishes us even when the waters just keep flowing and flowing? What is it that our roots can grab on to? What do they want to be connected with? What creates our security and stability? The deepest and most profound pain we experience brings us back into our roots. Where have we come from? Who are we really? What beliefs stand in the way of those answers? Pull them out. Question and prune.

There is choice in every moment, and so our power is never anywhere but here and now. Remember this affirmation when you identify a desire, and build on it with even more affirming statements: "This is my garden," "I have every right to its fruits," "My garden is loved, cared for, and will be even stronger next season," and "If I have little now, I will surely have much after such a rain, and if my seeds should wash away, I'll simply reach into my bag where I hold more and plant again. There will be enough to eat and enough to share."

Let the seasons and cycles of your life move you. You are worthy of abundance, understanding, and opportunities to share your uniqueness with this world. You're not missing anything; you're just growing into something.

I Am Letting Go

If there's one thing we are guaranteed to learn in this life, it is how to completely relinquish all personal control and let absolutely everything go. Unfortunately, many of us don't learn this until the moment of our death. But we don't have to wait so long, and if we realized the power in letting go, we wouldn't choose to wait another moment. Use the affirmation "I am letting go" to die a million times to each emerging version of the self you long to become. Yes, like all death, this work deals in the realms of grief and loss. But it's natural! There is nothing to be feared or avoided.

Trust that you can feel it all and it won't kill you; it will only take what you no longer need to carry. To let go is to let life take over. To let go is to trust that there is something larger than the little you. Something that moves you, animates you, loves you, and creates you. This life energy is capable of directing you toward fulfillment far beyond your wildest imaginings if you let it. This is the energy that can restore your hope, passion, and purpose and remind you that you are worthy of forgiveness.

What are you willing to lose in order to become everything? What will you give up to create something that shines with the light of your pure value? Are you willing to get uncomfortable? I have created human beings four times, and I can tell you this: Death is uncomfortable. Birth is uncomfortable. One always leads to the other, and letting go is a requirement of both. In fact, the process of death and birth could really be seen as one thing, as we die to the old and become the new.

Just as death won't let you take your favorite shirt or your "World's Best Dad" coffee mug, neither will life permit you to take all of your favorite things along with you into the new version of yourself. It's okay. You are allowed to feel whatever you feel about it as you are learning to let go.

Sometimes what we leave behind hurts, and sometimes it feels like a great relief. Usually, it's both. We see old stories, beliefs, and wounds come up to the surface to wave goodbye on their way out. Every step we take along our new path to authentic selfhood is a step away from what held us back. We walk, one pace at a time, into a life that is no longer limited by our limited beliefs. We recognize, over and over again, in a billion tiny ways and a few big ones, that the only thing we get to take with us, ever, is the most fundamental aspect of us, the one who is experiencing. And it's the only thing we ever really had.

Use the affirmation "I am letting go" to declare your trust in life's process as it meets your intention to live fully and strips away all that doesn't resonate with love. You will find yourself lighter, quite literally made of more light. You will shine on all that benefits from your illumination, bringing meaning to the world as it is seen by you in the way that only you can see it. You will find that becoming is not so much about acquiring more as it is about letting go.

PART 3
Aftermation

Welcome to the beginning. Each of these affirmations is endless. Each time you bring these words to life, you create an entirely new awareness. Something never before lived becomes alive through you. An experience comes to life that can only be had by you and only in the moment in which you are having it. It is incredibly special and exceptionally powerful to do anything with intention. Words, as directors and movers of energy, can be tools in our lives if only we choose to use them with the power and responsibility we are innately equipped with. There is never too much power for you to handle, never any reason to be afraid of yourself. Despite what you have been taught about your ability or lack thereof, you are capable of using words in a way that infuses your life with deep meaning and powerful purpose. Use these statements again and again to invite a new experience each time. You will never meet the same affirmation twice. Just check in with your feelings, thoughts, and emotions each time you read one, and you'll see you are an entirely different person than the last time that these words arrived to you.

Remember the protocol outlined in part one of this book. It is simple and profoundly useful. You'll continue to use this method each time you read this book or work with these affirmations in any context. I know we are not used to things being so simple; we really want things to be hard so they feel worth it. We have some deeply rooted stories about effort and how it is tied to meaning. This is a part of what we are rewriting through this work. When our effort is mobilized with the intention of self-growth, love, and health, it behaves differently than we are used to. What previously felt like pulling teeth transforms into a joyful process. As much as your mind tries to make any of this more complex, please remember, this work is mind-blowingly simple, to the point that the mind might have quite a bit to say about it!

During the process of writing this book, I was realizing all of these concepts in my own life on deeper and deeper levels. One night in particular as I was pacing back and forth across my bedroom floor holding my thirty-pound, very uncomfortably sick baby boy in an attempt to remind him that sleep was a viable option, I had a great moment of realization. It is worth saying again, although I've said it many times: Motherhood is the greatest gift in my life. Not only because I get to experience four divine beings who made their way through me to exist here. Not just because I get to feel the most immense love in the world every single day of my life. Not even because the joy they bring me is immeasurable and there's nothing I'd rather be doing on this planet. All of this would be enough, but they bring me something more. They bring me challenge. They bring me into the depths of my being, gasping for air. They take and take, and when I think there is nothing more I could possibly have to give, they see my desperation and they ask for more. As they should; they know what they deserve, and they know who I am. They know that I am endless. They invite me to challenge everything that says I'll run out, that says I can't do it, that says I'm not strong enough, that says there's no more.

What I hope you know now, after reading this book at least once, is that challenge is a great opportunity for alchemy, for growth, and to experience the ever-increasing clarity in remembering who we are. Challenge, no matter its disguise, knows our power and will accept nothing less than a full display—one so magnificent that we can no longer deny it. It asks us to show up for ourselves, for our dreams, and for love as love. It asks us to become stronger than the weaker means of motion. It requires us to walk in a faith that exists beyond fear and come all the way home.

Nearly tipping into the bed, the chair, the rug, anything that could hold me, I continued to pace, and my little one continued to ask more of me. I was alone with my thoughts and this being who couldn't share his, and suddenly, I remembered once again my power to choose.

I could choose to complain. I could choose to give voice to the part of me that ached, that was tired of having four sick children, that had a long day, that just desperately wanted to get something done other than this. I could have chosen to feed the flame of anger as it arose within me, but this moment, this quiet moment, didn't call for the spark of change that anger offers. And in my awareness of my thoughts as they tumbled down the long hallway of my mind, I could see each one and how it bumped into the next, giving it a little more oomph than the one before it. I felt each emotion as its companion thought drew it to the surface. I watched as the old walls offered their memories, their patterns, their "do it like this again." I chose to notice, and then I chose where to direct my attention.

This moment called for me to be soft, present, and patient. I knew this by looking into the mirror of my son. So, I chose it. I chose the words that would support myself in that moment, and I spoke in a whisper, "I am right on time," followed by, "There is enough time." Everything would get done, or maybe not; either way, I was where I was needed. I chose acceptance. I chose to trust that I was a part of something greater, and my desire to meet my need for rest was so beautifully human and so valid but also so small. I reminded myself that I was being lived by life and that life itself had my back. I chose to make it true by accepting it as such. I chose words that stimulated thoughts and subsequent emotions that calmed me and restored my energy. I stepped right into the chain reaction and directed it toward gratitude—not by accident, not because something wonderful happened, not even because I was feeling good or happy, but because I chose it. I chose it because it felt like love to choose it.

I didn't write this book because you need it; I wrote it because I need it. I need to know that there is a way for me to take what I am silently doing during these long nights and create something meaningful for myself and the ones I get to share this life with. I wrote it entirely selfishly to meet my need to create something nourishing for the world. I wrote it because I, personally, desire to see the people around me thrive.

See what I am getting at here? When we resonate with love, our deep personal desire is inherently selfless. Love is naturally supportive to the whole, and it is safe to trust that. So, I encourage you with everything that I am to follow your own heart and trust that you are creating something needed. You are needed. You matter, and I love you. Thank you for reading this book; you give it meaning.

PART 3

LAST, A NOTE FOR ANYONE WHO IS CONTEMPLATING LEAVING

Let the words of this book give you hope. You might think that as a mother of four my highest commitment in life is to my children, or as an artist that my greatest dedication is to my work. The truth is that through the challenges of my life I was invited to commit to something infinitely simpler: I was asked to commit solely to choosing to stay alive. To choose life through everything and anything that I experience. To let my death come naturally as it will but never by my own hand. This alone is enough. Life can work with us as long as we continue to be alive.

I know what it feels like to be in immeasurable pain, and I understand wanting to make it stop. Sometimes even the pain of confusion or shame is enough to make life unbearable. But what if the story changes and you're not being punished and you're not running out of time and you're most certainly not hopeless? What if your pain can become a neutral sensation? What if you remember who you are and it's not who you thought? What if you can heal whatever feels absolutely broken? What

if from this moment on you take the pressure off and just live life as an experiment? What if now and as many times as you need, whether you know what it means yet or not, you simply commit to live this life as love and see what changes? What if you commit to the experiment of staying alive? What if something unexpected happens? What if you are worth the risk of continuing to try? Whatever you believe in or don't, please open your heart, bring these words along with you as a companion into the unknown, and please just *stay*.

To those of you without whom this book would not exist and I would not be who I am:

Thank you to both of the fathers of my four children, who have helped my dreams come true in so many ways, including supporting me in having the time to write this book.

Thank you to Tom Mahoney whose love and poetry kept me going through so many of my dark days and met me in the light on my brightest.

Thank you to Tim Miejan who gave me a chance, a column, a connection with community and the space to begin to develop this book over my eighteen months writing for *The Edge* magazine.

Thank you to Diane Rubright for completely changing my life.

Thank you to Masonic Children's Hospital for my son.

Thank you to my mother and father for creating me and loving me, and whose lineage I am so grateful to both carry and unwind. And to my stepmother for teaching me even more about unconditional love.

Thank you to my siblings, my nieces and nephews, cousins, aunts, and uncles for inspiring me by being exactly who you are.

ACKNOWLEDGMENTS

Thank you to my ancestors who have stepped with me into every shadow and sat with me around the fire of our collective heart.

Thank you to my guides for teaching me how to write and rewrite my own stories.

Thank you to my future self for reaching your hand back to me and pulling me forward into the woman who wrote this, who shared this and who has so much more to share.

Thank you to my past self for being so, so brave. I love you.

Thank you to my friends who have loved me and supported me through all of the stories within these pages and so many more that I have yet to tell. Thank you for your hand on my back during my tears. Thank you for wiping the dirt from my feet and covering me with your most sacred blanket on the rainiest night, in the brightest tipi. Thank you for your music, for your warm cups of tea, for leaving the light on, and for asking me to come in.

Thank you to my children, who I live for and who I write for.

Thank you to my incredible team at Llewellyn who showed me it is safe to trust my precious work in your sturdy hands. You met me with honesty, collaboration, expertise, clear communication, and compassion every step of the way.

And thank you, reader, for being as much a part of this story as I am.

TO WRITE TO THE AUTHOR

If you wish to contact the author or would like more information about this book, please write to the author in care of Llewellyn Worldwide Ltd. and we will forward your request. Both the author and publisher appreciate hearing from you and learning of your enjoyment of this book and how it has helped you. Llewellyn Worldwide Ltd. cannot guarantee that every letter written to the author can be answered, but all will be forwarded. Please write to:

Mama Rose
℅ Llewellyn Worldwide
2143 Wooddale Drive)
Woodbury, MN 55125-2989

Please enclose a self-addressed stamped envelope for reply, or $1.00 to cover costs. If outside the U.S.A., enclose an international postal reply coupon.

Many of Llewellyn's authors have websites with additional information and resources. For more information, please visit our website at https://www.llewellyn.com.